INTRODUCTION

If you want to learn to draw heart-pumping, turbo-charged action heroes on the cutting edge of the comic book industry, then buckle up because we're going to break the speed limits on this ride.

You're going to learn how to draw alluring alien women, high-tech costumes, and unearthly villains. You'll learn how to draw the best flying poses; how to draw cyborgs; how to draw the muscles of the action hero; how to draw backgrounds; shading; silhouettes; how to stage a scene—you name it, it's in here.

You also get two authentic blank comic books with the panels already drawn in, so you can create your own comics. It comes with an HB pencil in a holder, which is standard for illustrators. And it's portable.

This book will show you the basics and more, because we're going after even bigger game—the techniques and tricks the pros use to create that gripping mood that doesn't let you put a comic book down.

With practice, passion, and a little flair, you can dramatically improve your artistic abilities. All it takes is desire and information. You've got the desire or you would never have read this far. As for the information, that's my job.

It's like everything else in life—if you want to be the best, you've got to go to the best, and this book has it. Some of the best artists in the industry have suited up to show you how it's done.

Yeah, I suppose you could grab a simpler, less challenging book, which will show you how to draw something easier that you'll master in no time. But your drawings won't look like the ones in this book. You'll end up frustrated, but you won't know why. After years of therapy, and thousands of dollars later, you will realize that it was that one fateful decision not to buy this book that caused your downfall. But by then it will be too late. As the nurse walks you down the hallway for your 4:30 dinner of creamed corn and kale, the rest of the residents will hear your terrible cry coming from the corridor, "If only I had purchased that really great but slightly more challenging book!"

It doesn't have to end like that.

How good do you want to be? It's up to you.

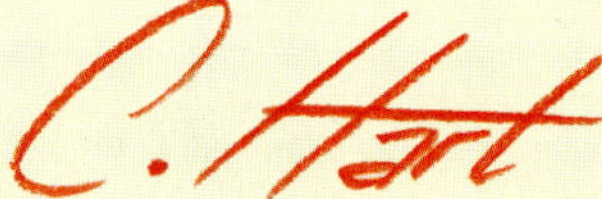

CONTENTS

THE EVIL ONES

What would a comic book be without the bad guys? Here are some of the different types of evil creatures you can create.

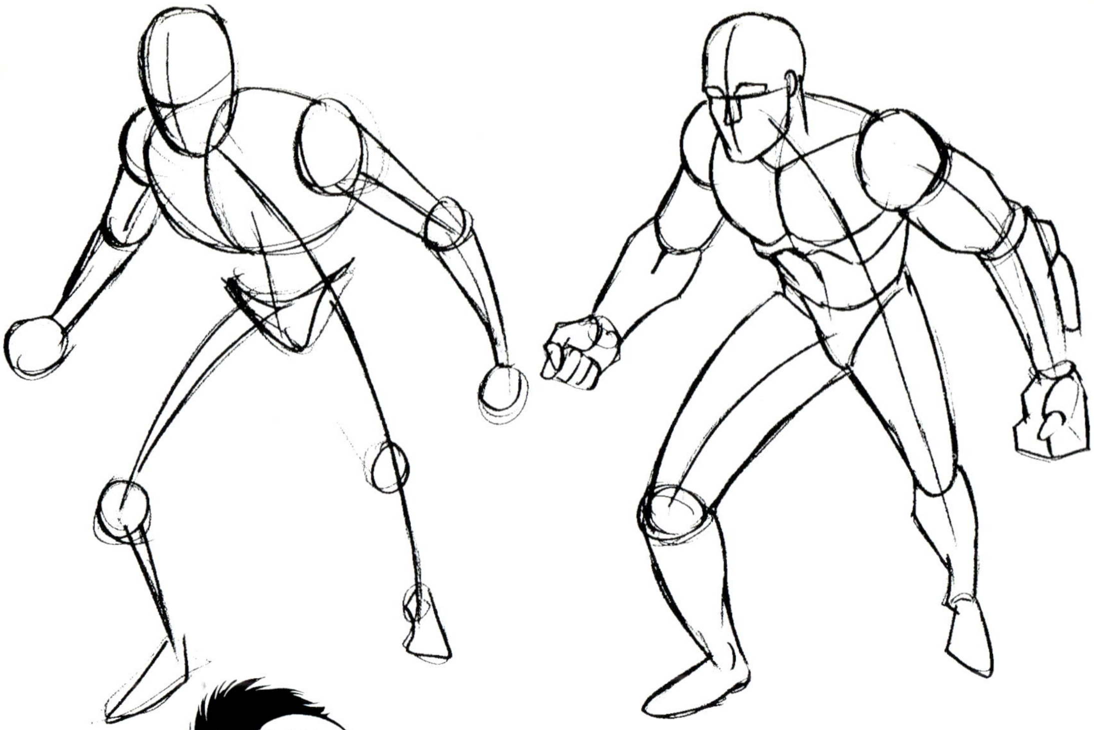

CYBORGS

Question: What do you get when you rip the outer coating off of a cyborg? Answer: a really ugly cyborg. They are creatures that are half-organic/half-machine. They have skin and hair, but underneath is pure microprocessor. The dramatic moment comes when a character you *thought* was human gets cut in a fight, and his hydraulic parts show. Visually, this is where you want your cyborg to end up, because it looks so *cool.* You can also start his story as a half-man/half-machine, as in this example.

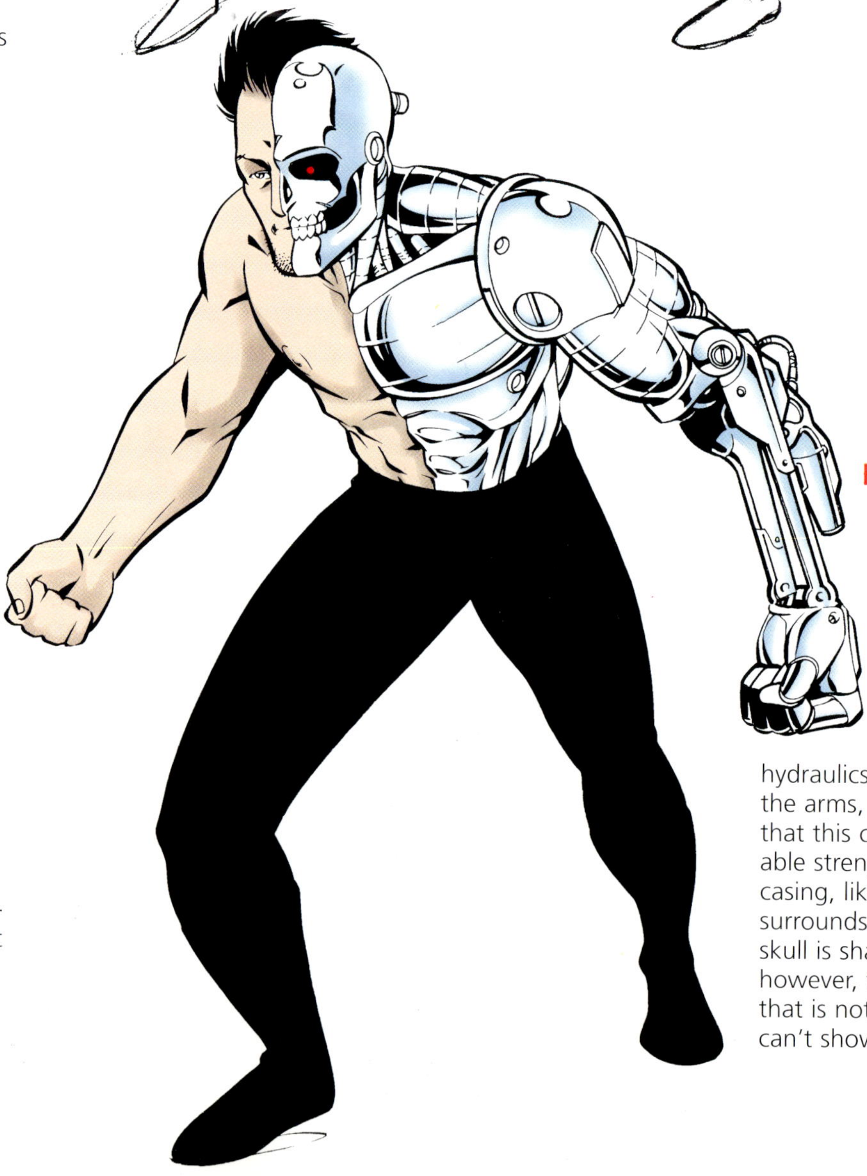

HINTS ON DRAWING THE CYBORG:
When you draw the cyborg, keep in mind that the machine half must look intricate and advanced, such as hydraulics (metal pumps) for the arms, to reinforce the idea that this creature has unbelievable strength. Shiny steel casing, like a metal shell, surrounds the body. The metal skull is shaped like a real skull; however, the side of the face that is not covered with skin can't show any expression!

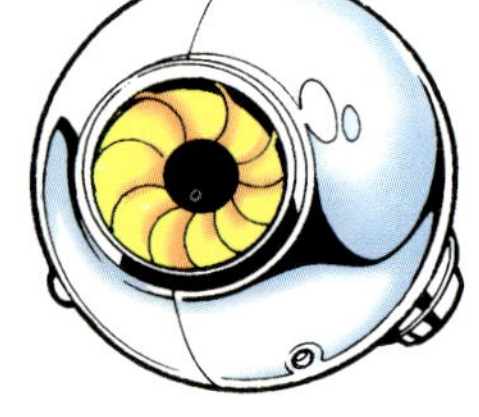

CYBORG EYES:
Cyborgs can have mechanical eyes that open and shut like a camera shutter. They are recessed, opening up and closing down, depending on the light, and how far it is trying to see.

THE ALIEN BABE

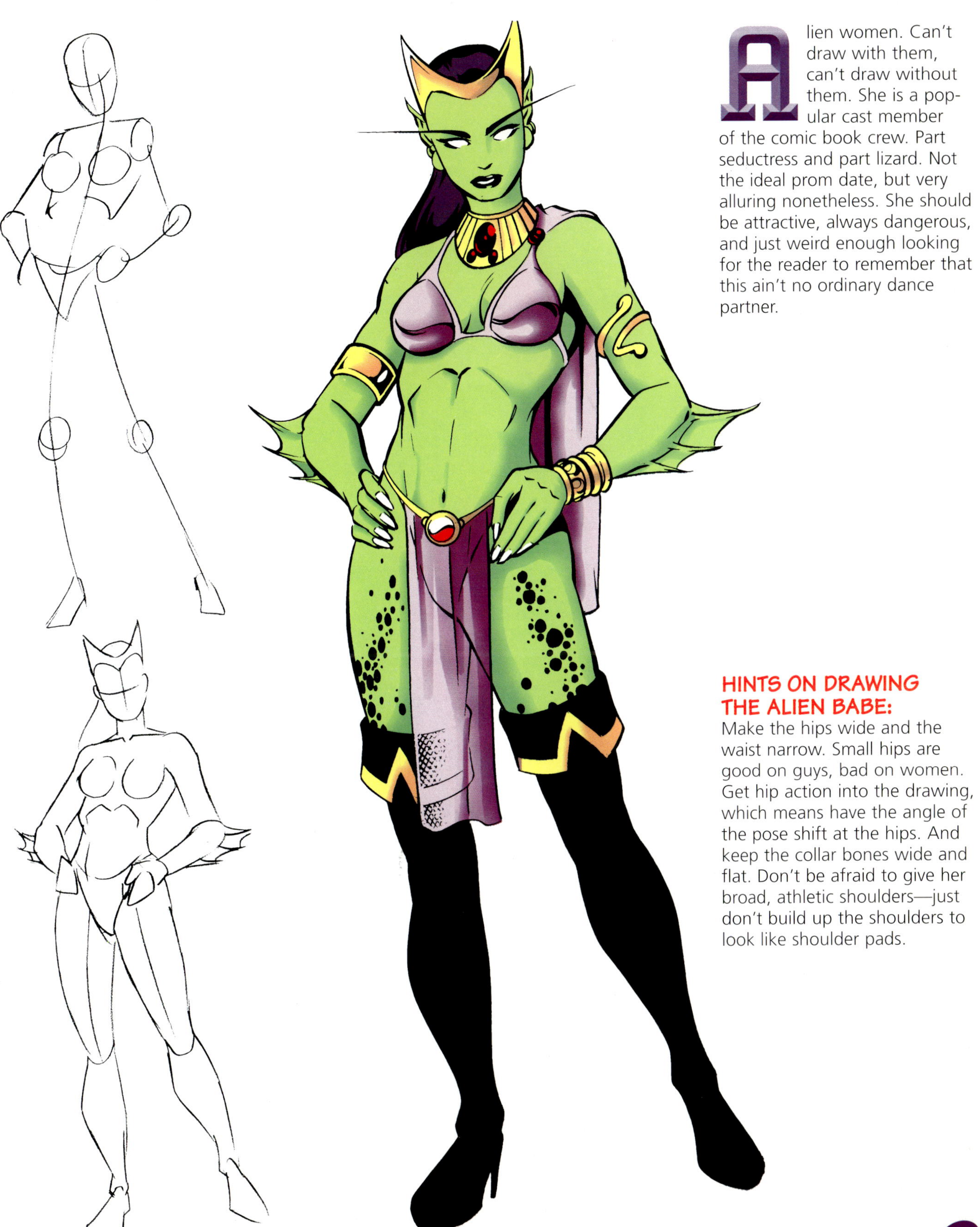

Alien women. Can't draw with them, can't draw without them. She is a popular cast member of the comic book crew. Part seductress and part lizard. Not the ideal prom date, but very alluring nonetheless. She should be attractive, always dangerous, and just weird enough looking for the reader to remember that this ain't no ordinary dance partner.

HINTS ON DRAWING THE ALIEN BABE:
Make the hips wide and the waist narrow. Small hips are good on guys, bad on women. Get hip action into the drawing, which means have the angle of the pose shift at the hips. And keep the collar bones wide and flat. Don't be afraid to give her broad, athletic shoulders—just don't build up the shoulders to look like shoulder pads.

MACHINES PROGRAMMED TO DESTROY

We're talking about a master killing machine. This guy makes a shark look like a puppy dog. The head is small because it doesn't have to do much thinking. It has only one task—to destroy. Look at what gets the emphasis—those massive claws. It can crush anything it gets it claws on. Its weakness is that it lacks agility and cunning.

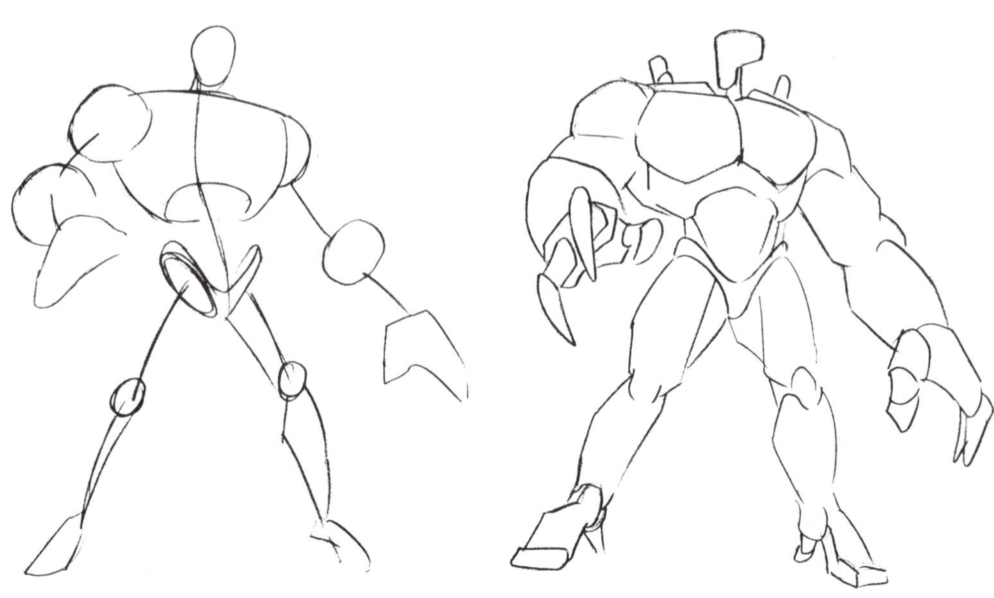

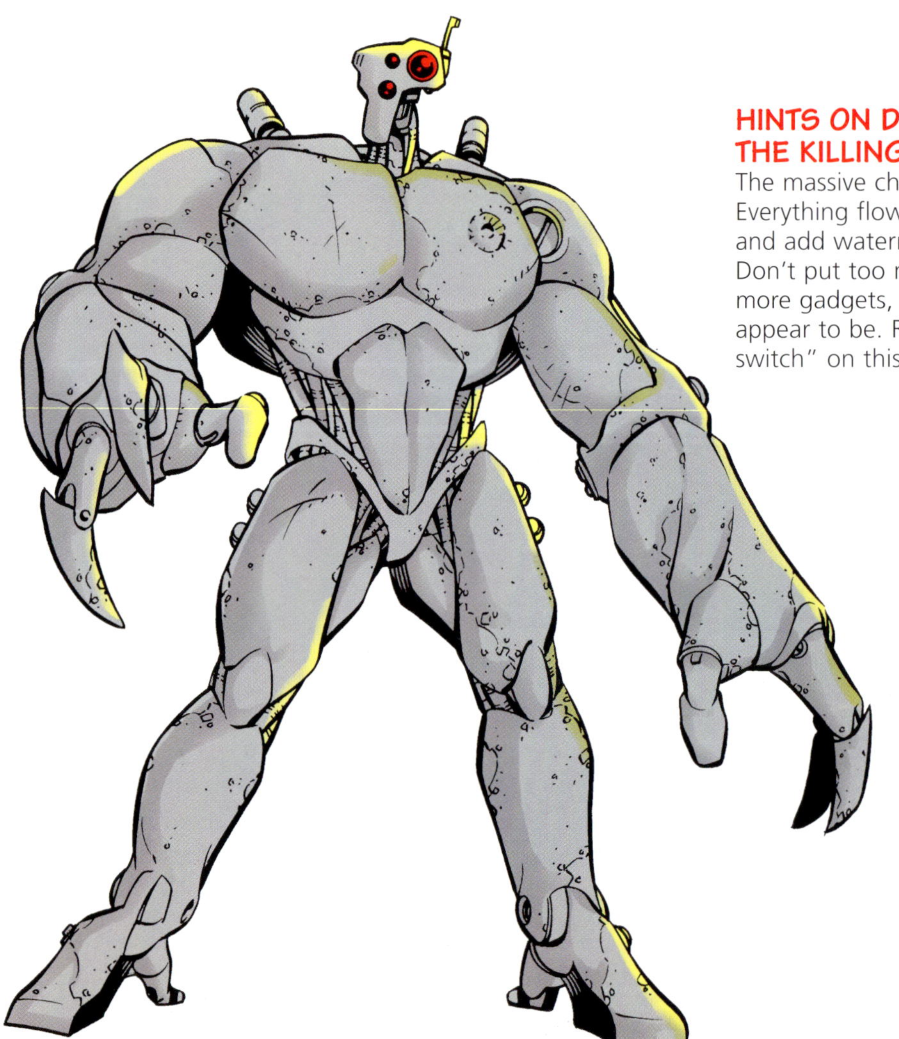

HINTS ON DRAWING THE KILLING MACHINE:
The massive chest dominates the frame. Everything flows from that. Draw it huge and add watermelon sized shoulders to it. Don't put too many doo-dads on him. The more gadgets, the more vulnerable he will appear to be. Remember, there's no "off switch" on this bad guy.

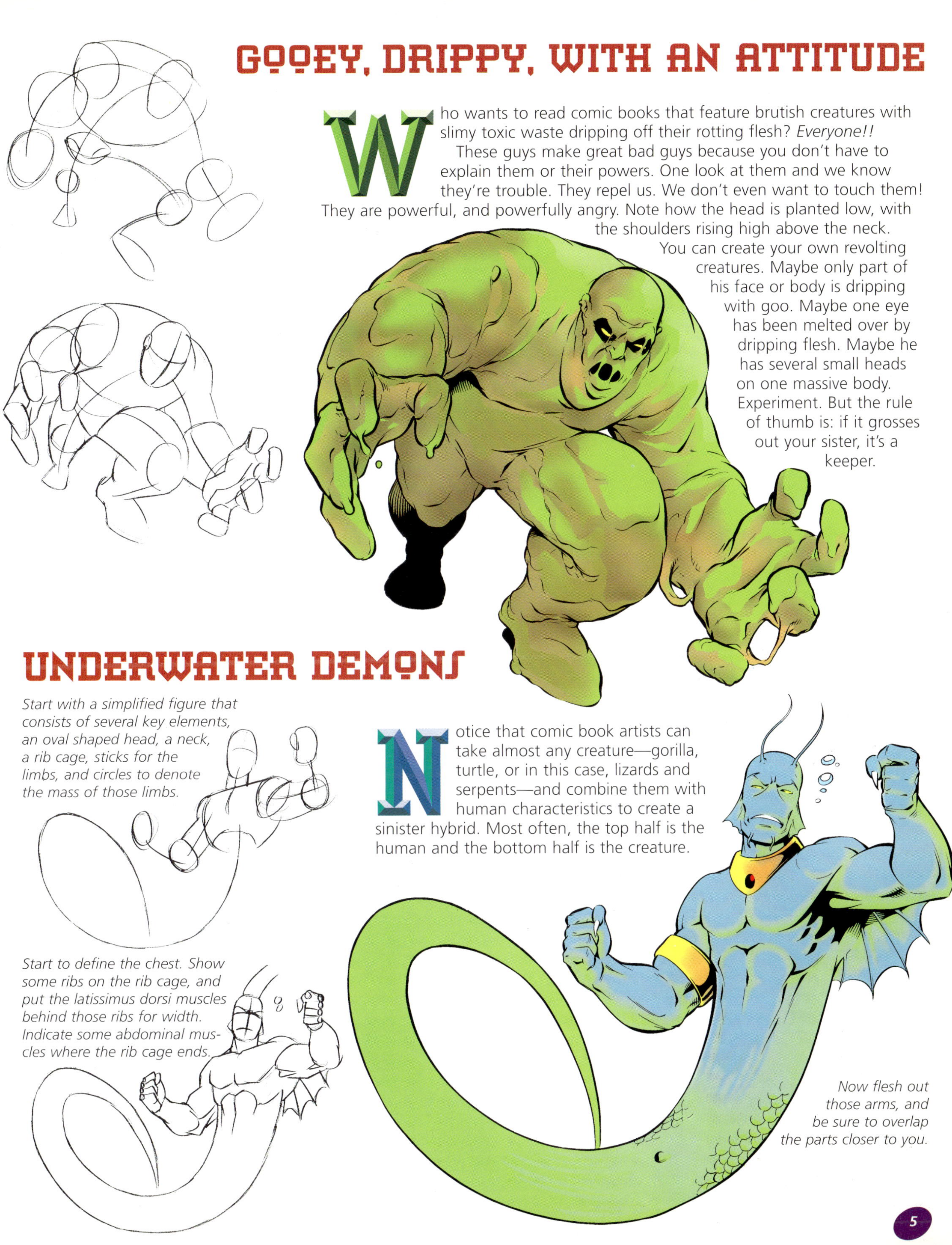

GOOEY, DRIPPY, WITH AN ATTITUDE

Who wants to read comic books that feature brutish creatures with slimy toxic waste dripping off their rotting flesh? *Everyone!!*

These guys make great bad guys because you don't have to explain them or their powers. One look at them and we know they're trouble. They repel us. We don't even want to touch them! They are powerful, and powerfully angry. Note how the head is planted low, with the shoulders rising high above the neck.

You can create your own revolting creatures. Maybe only part of his face or body is dripping with goo. Maybe one eye has been melted over by dripping flesh. Maybe he has several small heads on one massive body. Experiment. But the rule of thumb is: if it grosses out your sister, it's a keeper.

UNDERWATER DEMONS

Start with a simplified figure that consists of several key elements, an oval shaped head, a neck, a rib cage, sticks for the limbs, and circles to denote the mass of those limbs.

Notice that comic book artists can take almost any creature—gorilla, turtle, or in this case, lizards and serpents—and combine them with human characteristics to create a sinister hybrid. Most often, the top half is the human and the bottom half is the creature.

Start to define the chest. Show some ribs on the rib cage, and put the latissimus dorsi muscles behind those ribs for width. Indicate some abdominal muscles where the rib cage ends.

Now flesh out those arms, and be sure to overlap the parts closer to you.

FUNNY BAD GUYS

Bad guys are the spice of comic books. Some guys are evil and scary. Some are evil and hilarious. Humor, judiciously placed, can make a scene even more dramatic, because it makes for more varied pacing. And storytelling is nothing without pacing.

Funny bad guys are bumbling, grandiose, and delightfully wicked. They relish their fantasies of world power and domination. They are the ones who got humiliated in front of their classmates by their grade school teacher, and committed the rest of their lives to making society pay for that humiliation. In other words, they're just like you and me.

EVIL SCIENTIST

The evil scientist wears a lab coat and has an impressive underground lab. Some evil scientists are depicted as bald with huge heads (to capitalize on the myth that people with big heads are smart), but I also like another variation: the crazy-eyed scientist with wild hair.

I like to make his torso top heavy, to give him an uneasy, lopsided appearance.

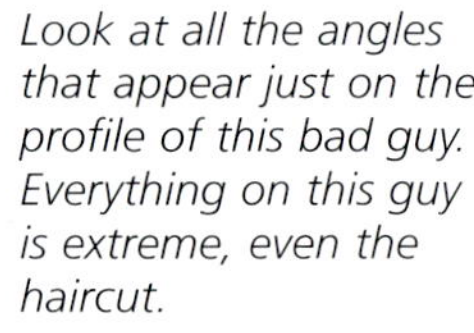

Look at all the angles that appear just on the profile of this bad guy. Everything on this guy is extreme, even the haircut.

BONE CRUSHING BULLIES

Unfortunately, some bad guys ate all their veggies and drank their milk when they were little, and grew up to be *big* bad guys. These powerhouses like to crush things. Give them extreme hairstyles, very angular features, and extra wide necks but small waists. Think of them as pit bulls without the tail.

This type of character can also work well as a dimwitted assistant to the mad scientist, but there is little loyalty among thieves, so eventually the bone crusher may decide he wants to stop taking orders and start running the show himself.

THE NERD

This is a typical bad guy "nerd." He's smart—sort of—but he thinks he's much smarter than he actually is. He hates children, so it's fun to put plenty of snotty, curious kids in his neighborhood to pester him. He usually wears glasses and is seriously lacking in fashion sense. By giving him skinny arms and a fat torso, his body takes on a humorous appearance. Funny bad guys are always building their own sinister progeny. Robots make good invention/companions. Give the robot an attitude too.

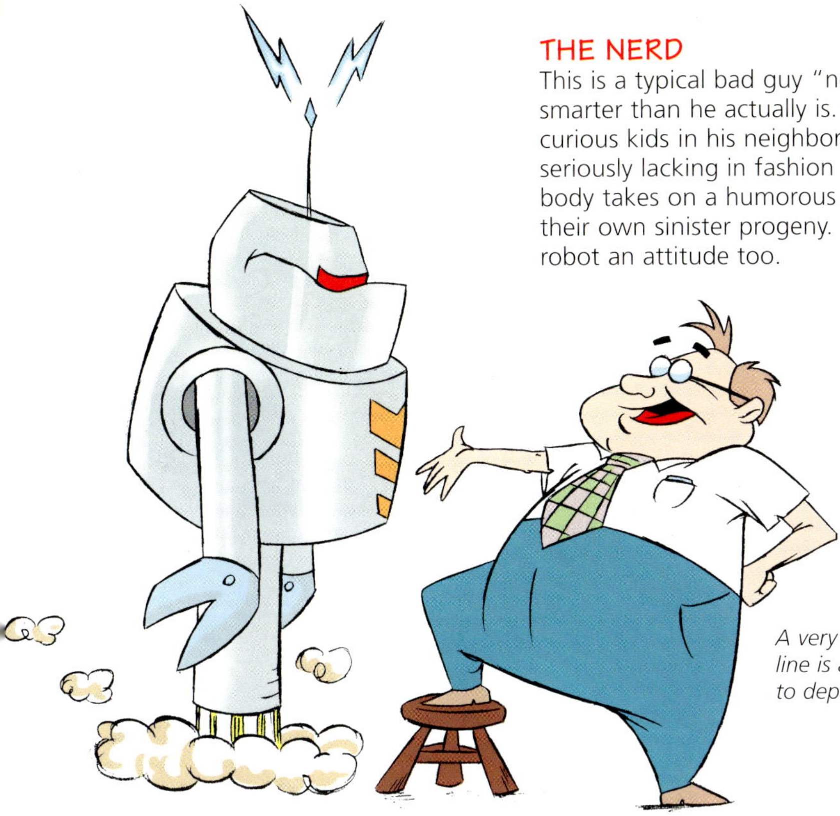

A very high belt line is a sure-fire way to depict a nerd.

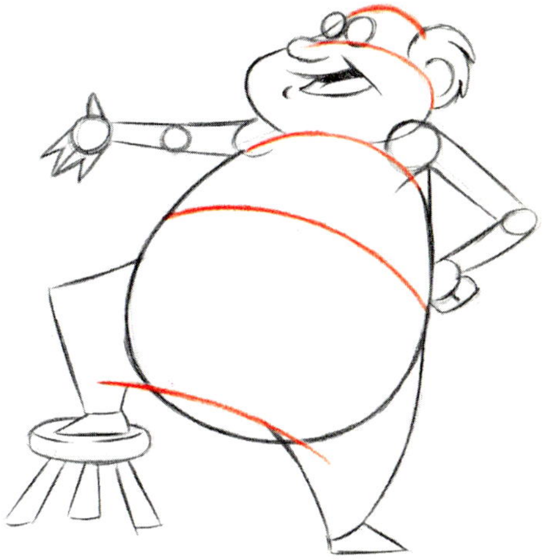

CRAZY GUYS

Insane guys are drawn with crazy poses and angles. To make your character look like he has only one oar in the water (metaphorically speaking), show his craziness by giving him insane poses depicted at weird angles.

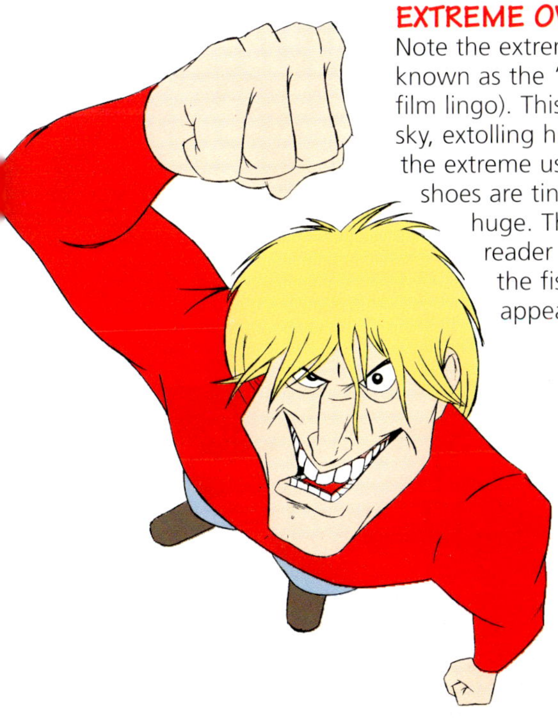

REAR ANGLE

This "morally challenged" scientist is bent on revenge. Sure, I could have drawn him from the front, but it pays to dig deeper and come up with more creative solutions. He is almost hidden by his hunched back, giving him a cowardly posture. Evil guys are always cowards, deep down.

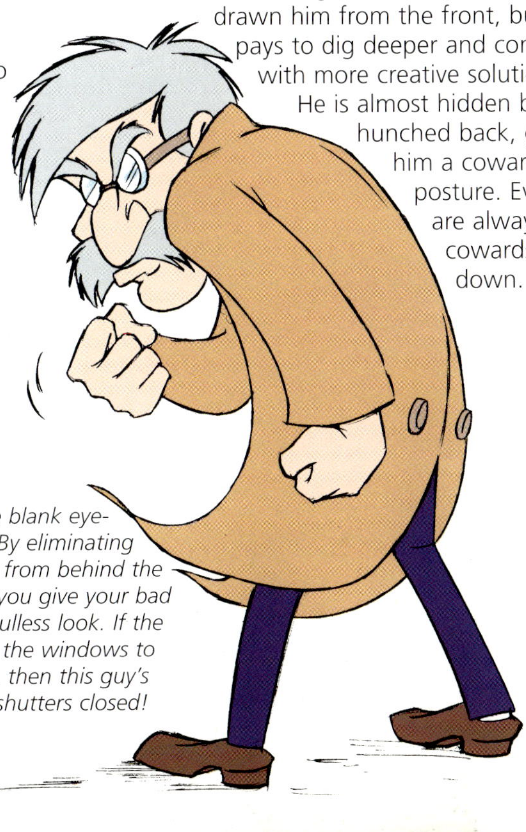

EXTREME OVERHEAD SHOT

Note the extreme overhead shot (also known as the "bird's eye view" in film lingo). This guy is ranting to the sky, extolling his evil ambitions. Note the extreme use of perspective. The shoes are tiny and the torso is huge. The fist closest to the reader appears larger, while the fist that is further away appears smaller.

Note the blank eyeglasses. By eliminating the eyes from behind the glasses, you give your bad guy a soulless look. If the eyes are the windows to the soul, then this guy's got the shutters closed!

CREATING THE HERO

HEAD IN PROFILE

The profile is the easiest head position to draw because you only have to draw one of everything. One eyebrow, one eye, one ear. So it's a good, quick angle with which to invent a new character. It also eliminates any foreshortening problems.

1. *In the first construction, we've established the outline. Notice how the line of the back of the neck changes angles as it becomes the base of the skull. See how the base of the skull travels in a diagonal line up to the crown of the head, then slopes down slightly to the forehead where it makes an abrupt angle downward to the chin. At the base of the chin, the line makes another sharp turn back to the front of the neck.*

2. *Now start to work on the interior features of the face. Sketch horizontal lines across the head as guidelines where you want to place the eyebrows, eyes, nose, and lips. Notice the indentations and protrusions of the face, which are most easily seen in the profile. There are indentations in the middle of the forehead, where it connects to the bridge of the nose, where the bottom of the nose meets the upper lip, and one just below the upper lip.*

3. *Work on the details only after you've done the preliminary constructions. If you spend more time on the construction, and less on the details, your drawing skills will improve much more quickly.*

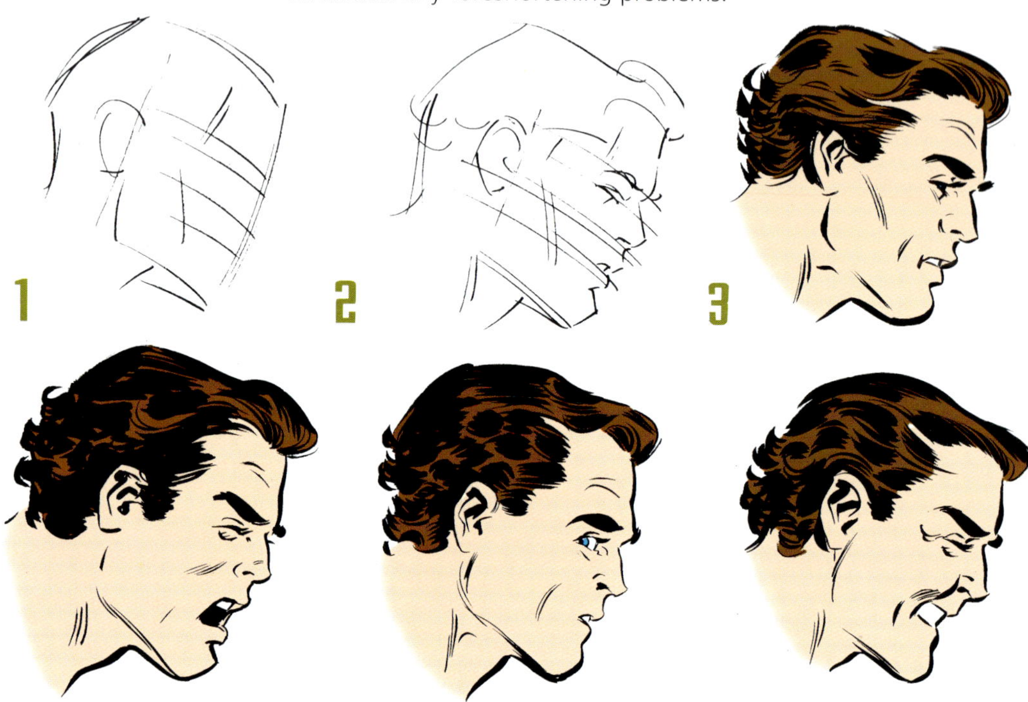

Note how the expressions of the character can change without altering the head construction.

HEAD ANGLES

When you draw a face in a 3/4 view, you have to spend a little more time on it, because you're balancing both sides of the face. One part of the face will be smaller than the other (the side closest to you is always larger). Also, be sure to define the cheek bones, which are more easily seen in this view.

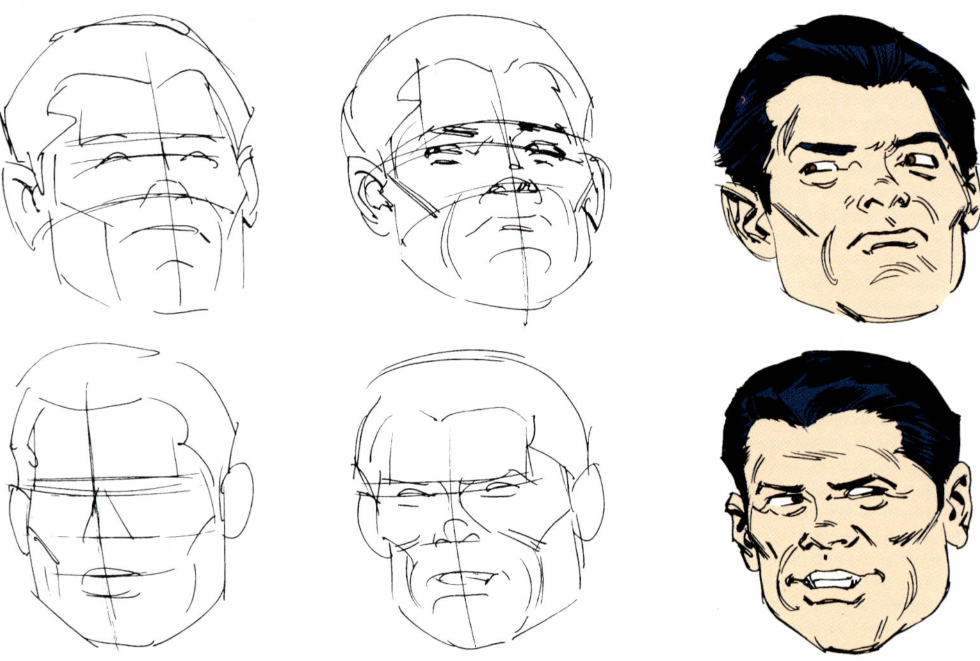

Continue to make small adjustment to the character until you've got it right.

DRAWING THE ACTION FIGURE'S BODY

Use a basic "V" shape for sketching out the torso. Then section it off at the chest, ribs, and waist.

Learning proportions takes time and practice. With experience, you will be able to "eyeball" a drawing and see where the body should be lengthened or shortened. But, in order to give you a head start, here are the classic proportions. Check them against you own characters, and adjust your drawings accordingly. Of course, not everyone is built this way, but comic books primarily use idealized physiques which adhere to these proportions.

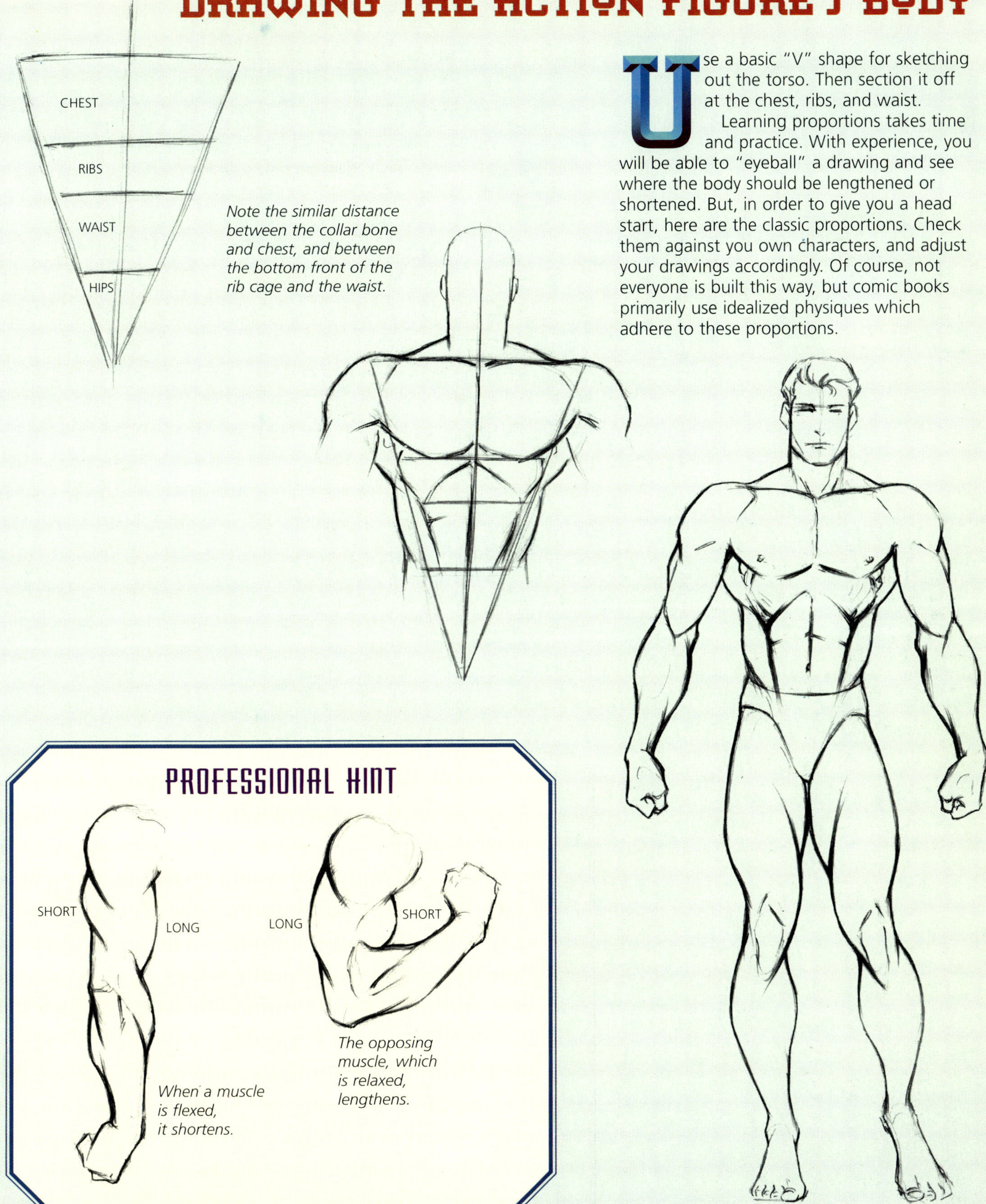

Note the similar distance between the collar bone and chest, and between the bottom front of the rib cage and the waist.

PROFESSIONAL HINT

When a muscle is flexed, it shortens.

The opposing muscle, which is relaxed, lengthens.

PROPORTIONS

How tall is the average person? The answer isn't 5 feet, 6 feet, or even 6½ feet tall. Artists use the head as the basic unit of measurement. The average person is approximately 7 heads tall. The crotch is generally the halfway point of the figure. But comic book action heroes are usually exaggerated, and are at least 8 heads tall. The extra height gives them their heroic stature. Note the numbers running along the vertical column. The dash along side each number represents the size of 1 head. The man is 8½ heads tall. The woman is 8 heads tall.

The line going from the base of the neck all the way down to the ground on each character is the center of gravity, also known as the "Atlas bone." A standing, stable human figure will have the Atlas bone directly over a point between the feet.

Proportions are directly related to its perspective, and everything is affected by perspective—people as well as buildings (see page 43 for more on perspective). The horizontal lines drawn over the figures above are merely guidelines that help the artist visualize the perspective of each character. Because each character is drawn in perspective, as they get farther away the converge to a common vanishing point, and subsequently appear to get smaller. That is why the guy's right foot appears to be lower than his left foot, and his left shoulder seems to be lower than his right.

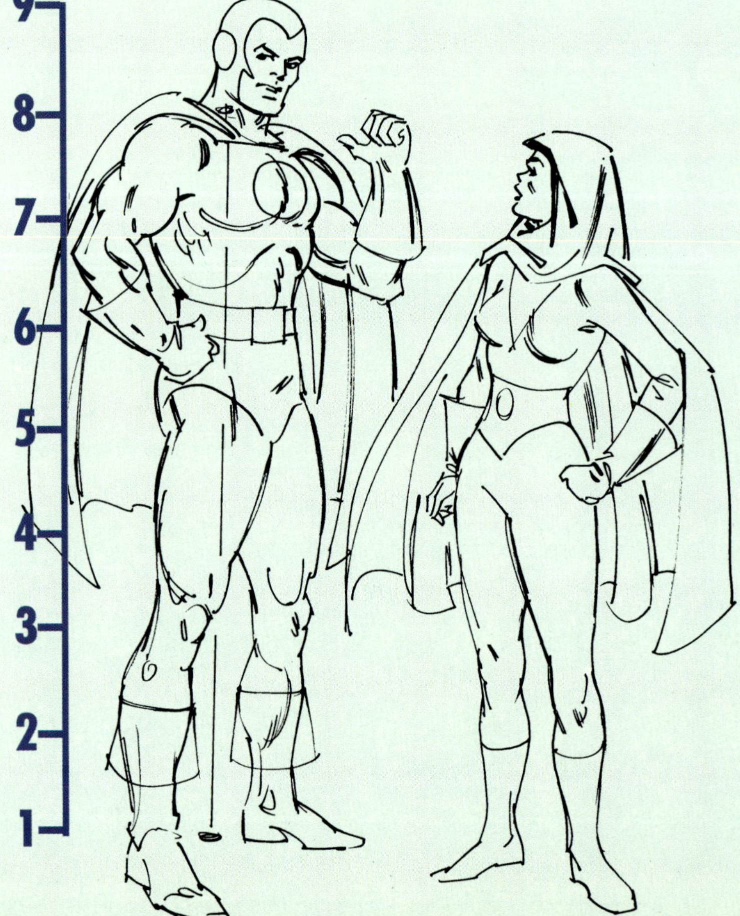

THE CENTER OF GRAVITY

When a character starts to run, he leans into the action, bringing his height down. Be aware of the changes in height that accompany various actions, whether it is as extreme as this, or as subtle as a bent knee.

The walking guy's center of gravity is directly below his lead foot. But the center of gravity for the running guy is about a foot or two in front of his feet, because he has shifted his weight out in front.

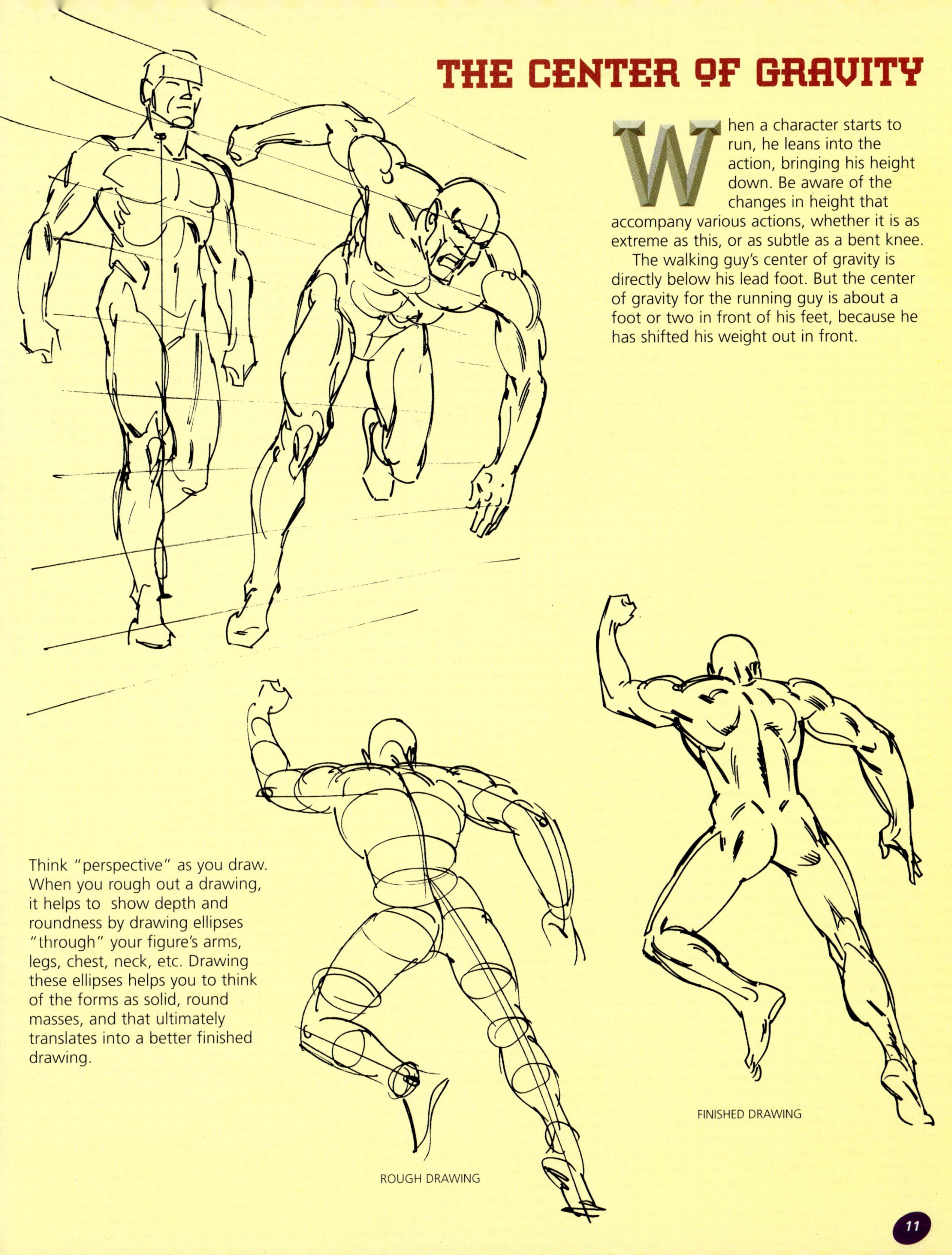

Think "perspective" as you draw. When you rough out a drawing, it helps to show depth and roundness by drawing ellipses "through" your figure's arms, legs, chest, neck, etc. Drawing these ellipses helps you to think of the forms as solid, round masses, and that ultimately translates into a better finished drawing.

FINISHED DRAWING

ROUGH DRAWING

RIPPLING MUSCLES

Your comic book characters should look like they spend endless hours pumping iron. But there's more to drawing muscles than adding "bumps" to the frame of a body. Study these examples to familiarize yourself with the various muscle groups. If a muscle stretches horizontally across the body (as in the chest muscles), but you sketched the striations as if they went up and down, it would look wrong, even to the unsophisticated eye.

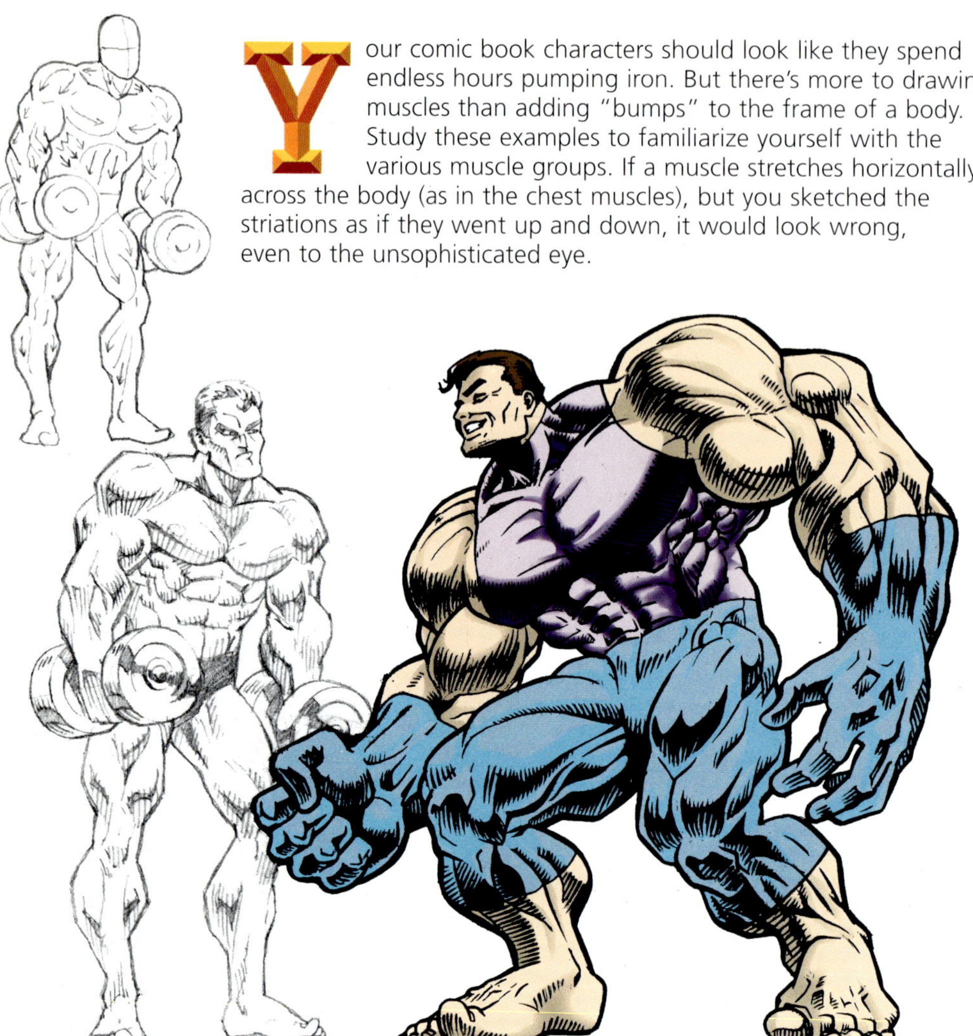

NORMAL HERO

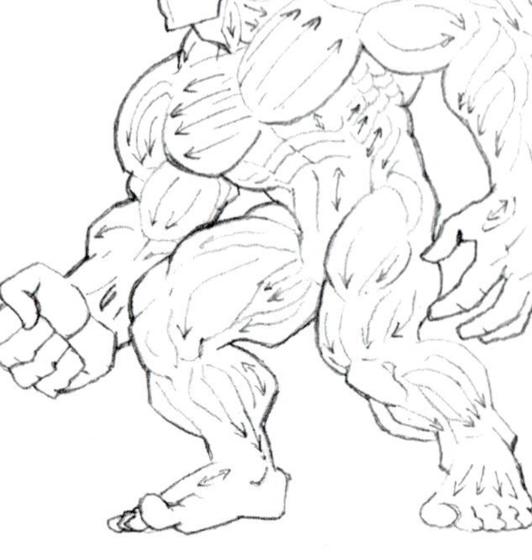

MASSIVE BRUTES

Gargantuan heroes and villains have muscles that really "pop." For these awesome creatures, you can invent new muscles by adding more layers and striations to the existing muscle groups. Note that the head does not increase in size along with the body.

INITIAL SKETCHES VS. FINISHED DRAWINGS

Look at the *initial* sketch of this karate-kicking character. Note how her shoulder blades, triceps, deltoids, and the creases at the hips are all clearly defined. But on the *final* sketch, some of the earlier definition has been left out, making her more attractive. A character doesn't need to have every muscle flexed in every pose.

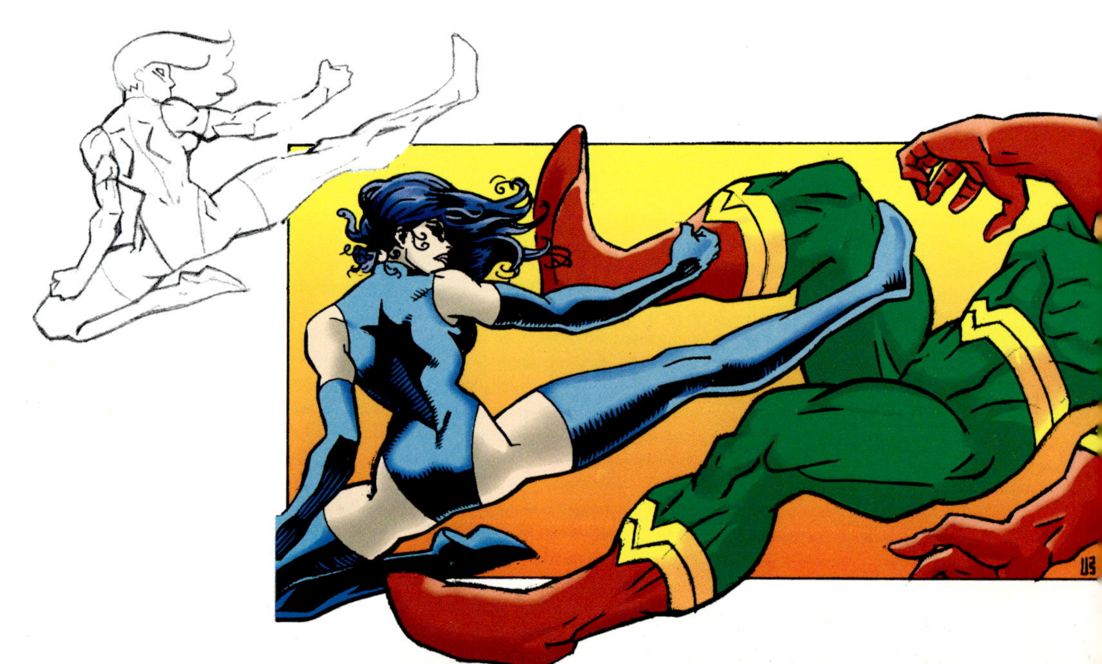

CRUNCHING

You can give your character a more dramatic look by positioning him or her so that part of the body "crunches" down on itself. Look at the guy running—you can feel the crunch of the muscles that cover the ribs (serratus anterior). The example of the animal-woman shows her left arm reaching up and over her head, crunching her body toward her right side. "Crunching" works much better than stiff poses.

FLEX AND RELAX

When one side of a muscle group is tense, the opposite side is relaxing. Granted, some comic book characters never look very relaxed, so everything is relative!

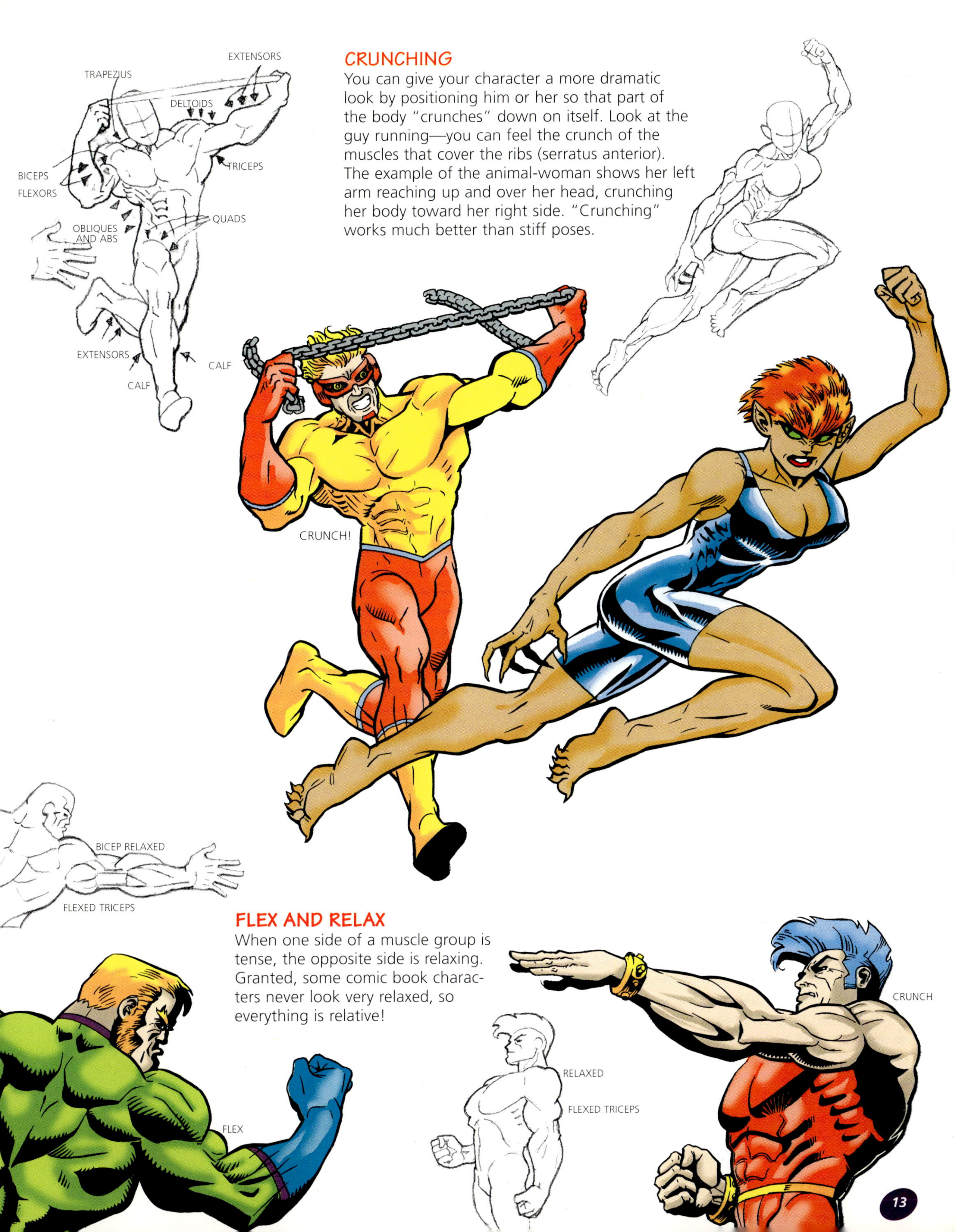

COSTUMES ON THE CUTTING EDGE

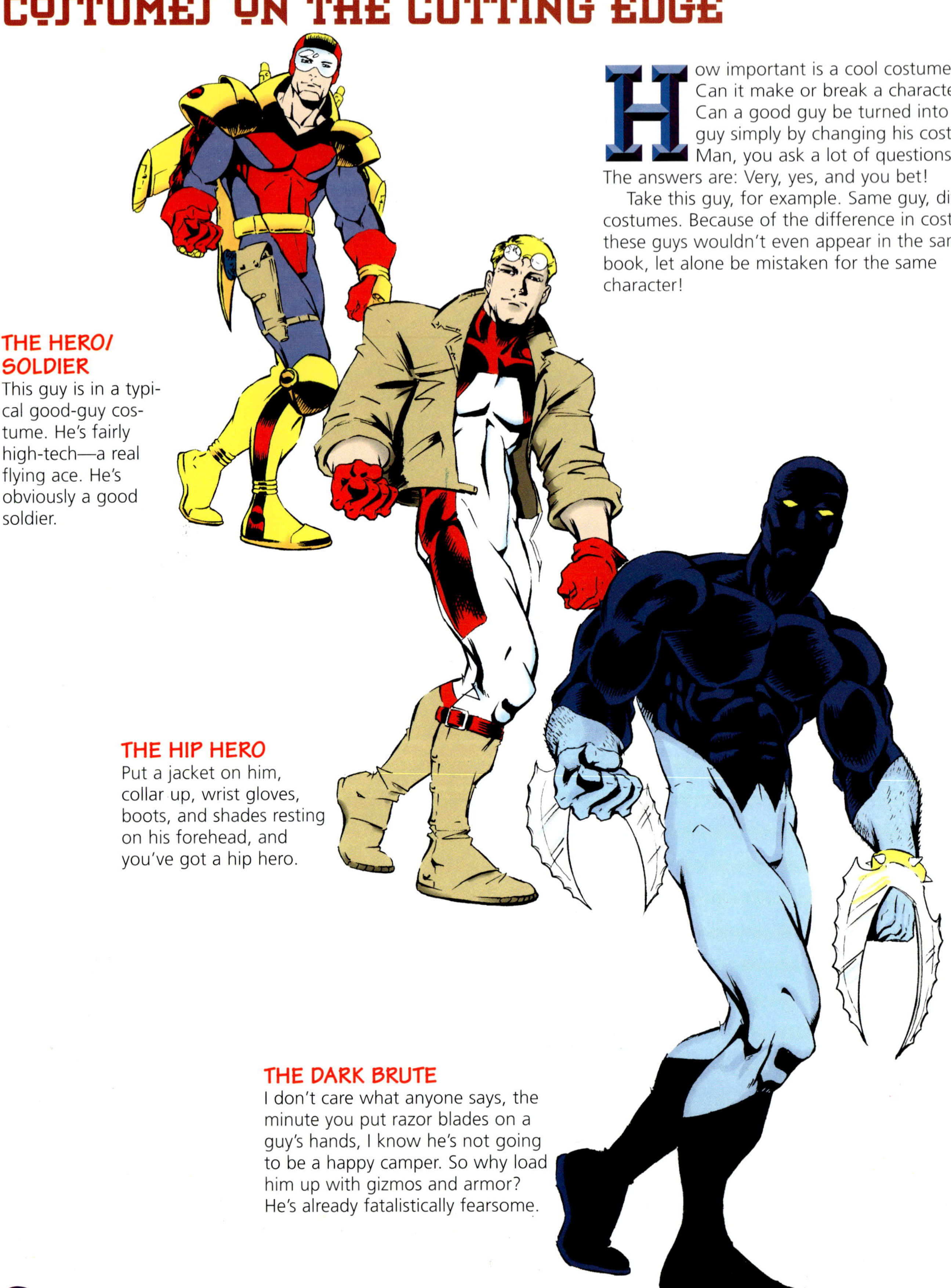

How important is a cool costume? Can it make or break a character? Can a good guy be turned into a bad guy simply by changing his costume? Man, you ask a lot of questions! The answers are: Very, yes, and you bet!

Take this guy, for example. Same guy, different costumes. Because of the difference in costumes, these guys wouldn't even appear in the same book, let alone be mistaken for the same character!

THE HERO/ SOLDIER
This guy is in a typical good-guy costume. He's fairly high-tech—a real flying ace. He's obviously a good soldier.

THE HIP HERO
Put a jacket on him, collar up, wrist gloves, boots, and shades resting on his forehead, and you've got a hip hero.

THE DARK BRUTE
I don't care what anyone says, the minute you put razor blades on a guy's hands, I know he's not going to be a happy camper. So why load him up with gizmos and armor? He's already fatalistically fearsome.

MASKS—THE FINISHING TOUCH

Masks are more than merely identity concealment devices. They add mystery, color, and excitement to a character. They can highlight a feature or hide one. Sometimes a mask has no utility, other than the fact that it looks good. Other times it has a purpose, affixed with high-tech devices, and sometimes it is part of a life-support system without which the character cannot live.

But remember one thing—almost all characters sooner or later take off their masks. Therefore, when you create a masked character, make sure you also design the face *without* the mask.

STANDARD MASK
Covers the face only

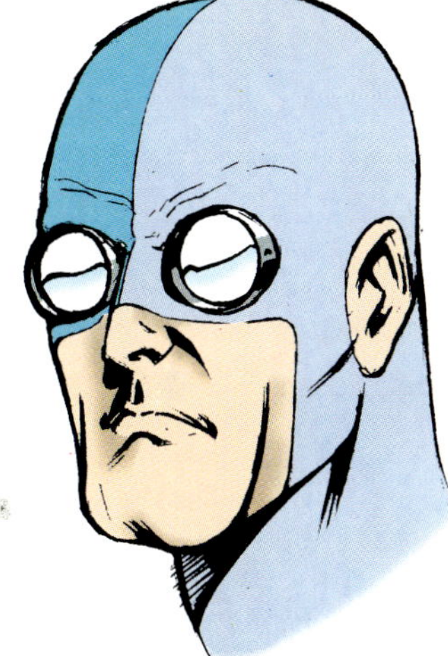

GOGGLED MASK
Covers head and neck

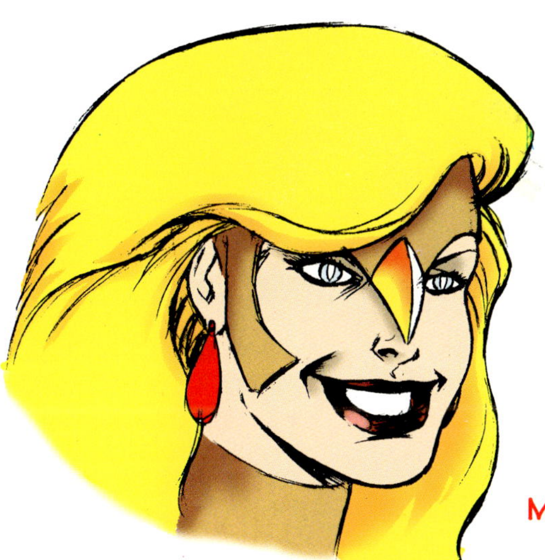

CROWN MASK
Gives a regal look to the character

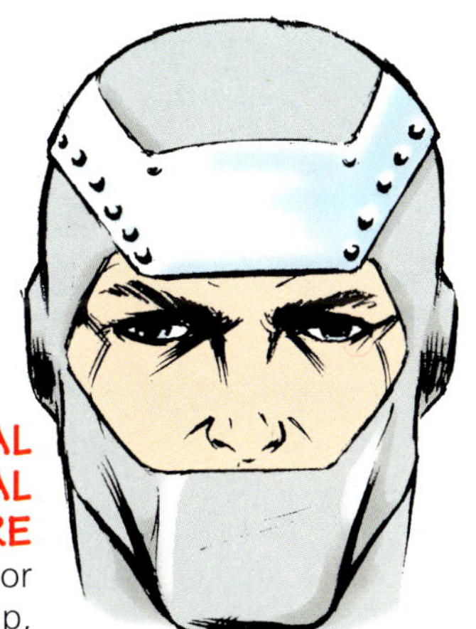

MINIMAL FACIAL EXPOSURE
Inconvenient for sipping soup, but looks good

TOTAL HEAD MASK
Meant to go with a total body shell costume

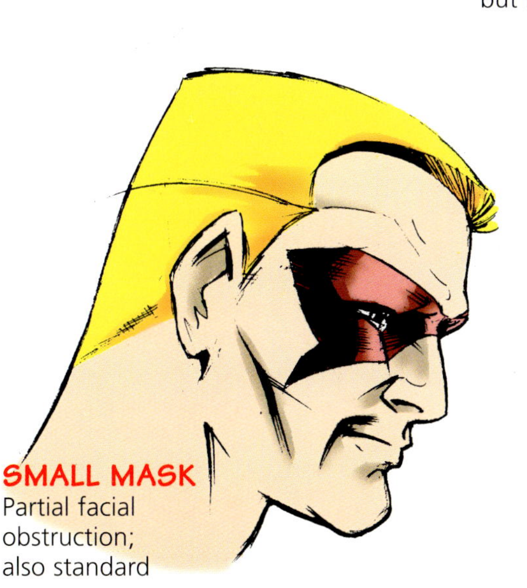

SMALL MASK
Partial facial obstruction; also standard

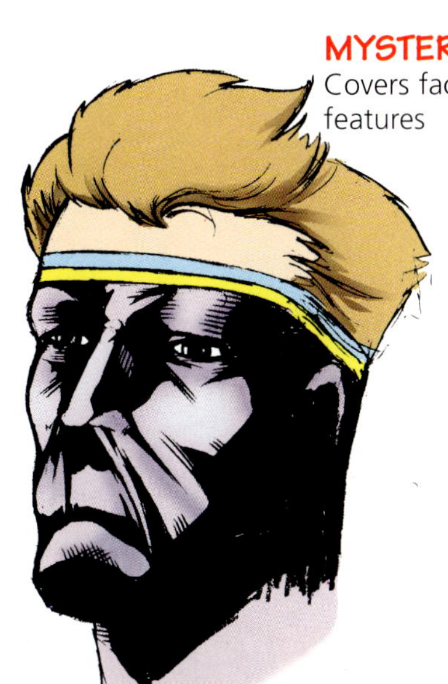

MYSTERIOUS TYPE
Covers facial features

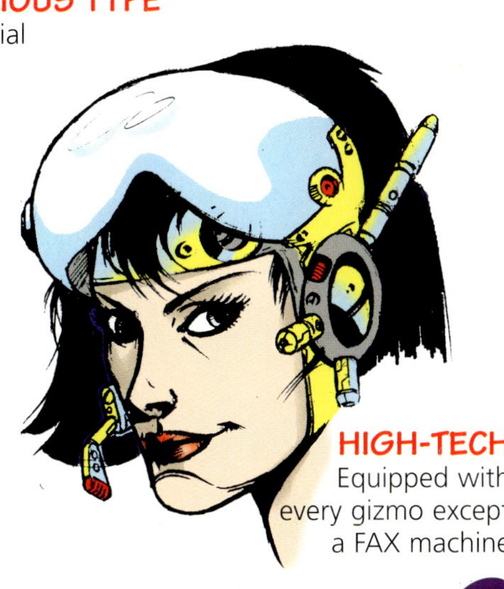

HIGH-TECH
Equipped with every gizmo except a FAX machine

DRAWING THE WOMEN

In drawing comics, you must continually reinvent your characters in a variety of poses to keep the reader's interest. Try drawing your female characters from these appealing angles. Notice that every pose conveys an attitude, no matter how subtle. It is more than a mere drawing. You get the feeling that each character has been caught in a moment. That's the key to good illustration.

When drawing the figure, it is best to exaggerate the feature. Comic books usually depict the men with extreme muscles and power, and the women with sex appeal and allure as well as power.

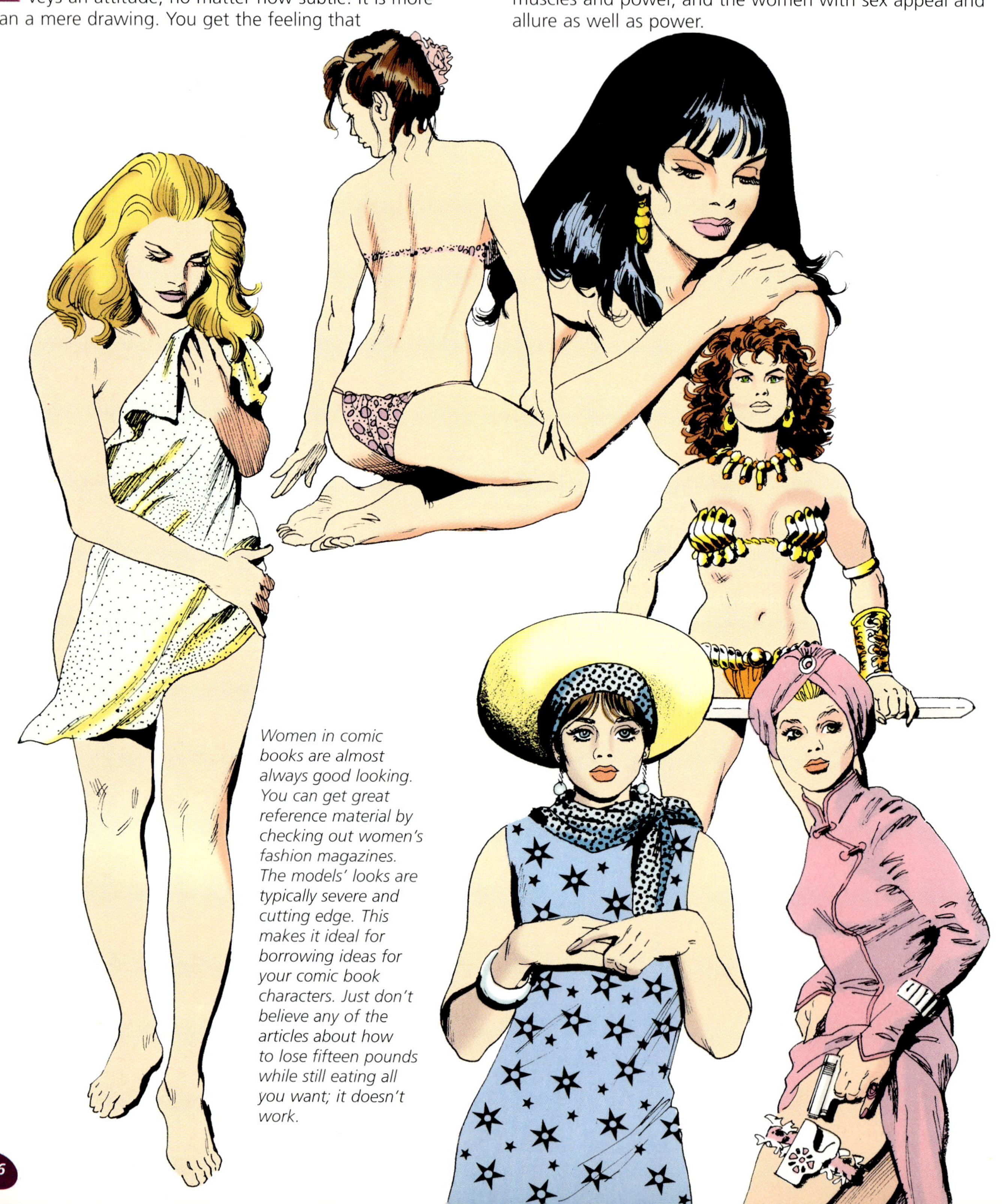

Women in comic books are almost always good looking. You can get great reference material by checking out women's fashion magazines. The models' looks are typically severe and cutting edge. This makes it ideal for borrowing ideas for your comic book characters. Just don't believe any of the articles about how to lose fifteen pounds while still eating all you want; it doesn't work.

THE FEMALE HEAD

It is very important to be able to draw the head from all sorts of angles so you can add variety to your comic book page. Remember that in addition to turning a head from side to side, people invariably also tilt their heads up and down, to the side and down, up and to the side, etc. Although the character is fairly well realized at this point, you should continue to make minor adjustments and small improvements.

THE HAIR
It must be casual, as if naturally fell that way. Don't make it look as if she spent hours working on it.

EYEBROWS
Naturally thick, tapering at the ends.

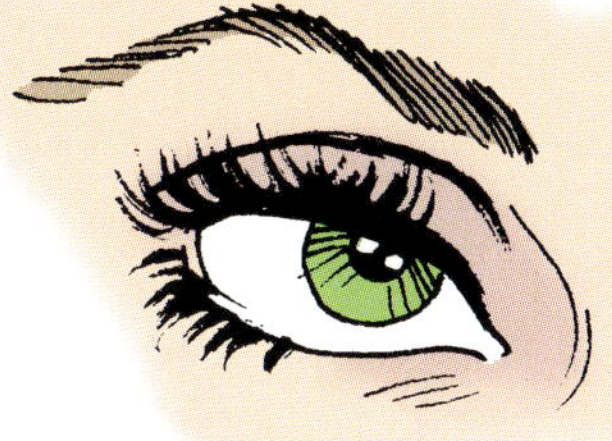

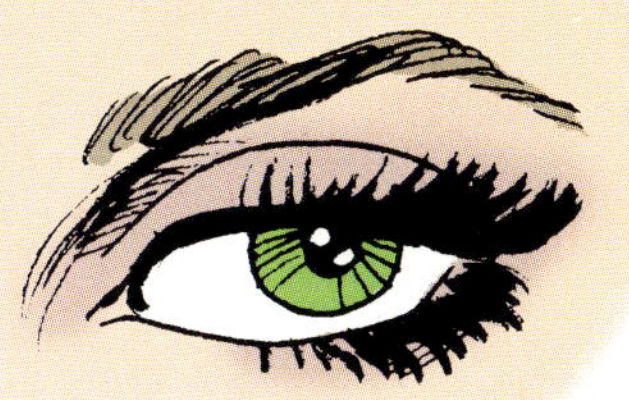

EYES
Large and expressive, just peaking out of thick lashes.

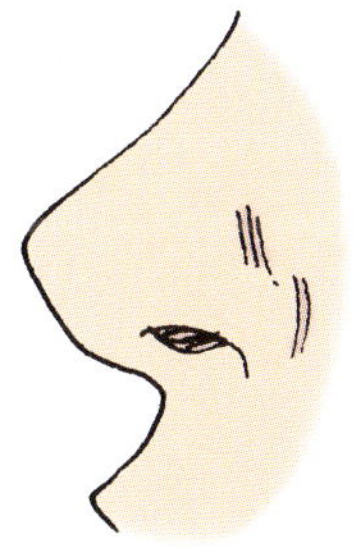

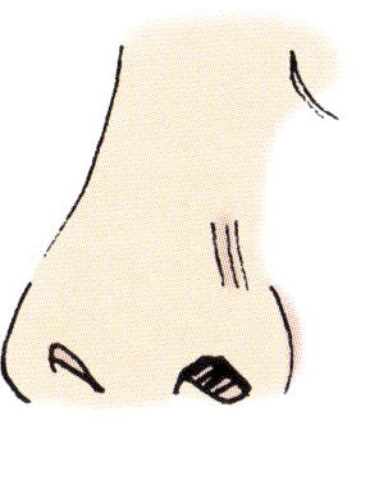

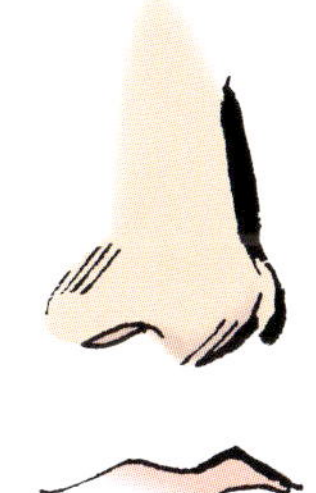

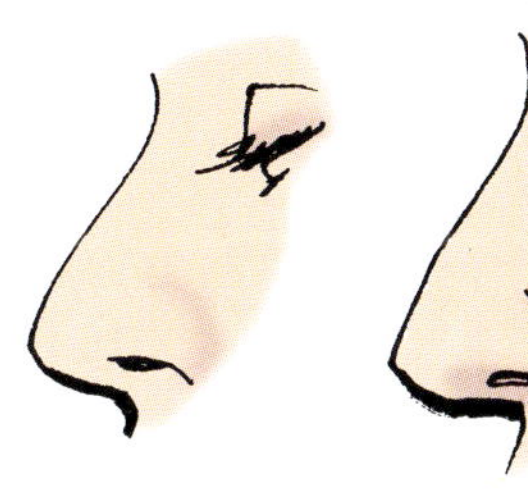

NOSE
Often small and turned up. Sometimes convex or even turned down in more dramatic characters. Here are some variations of the nose that were toyed with before settling on the final version.

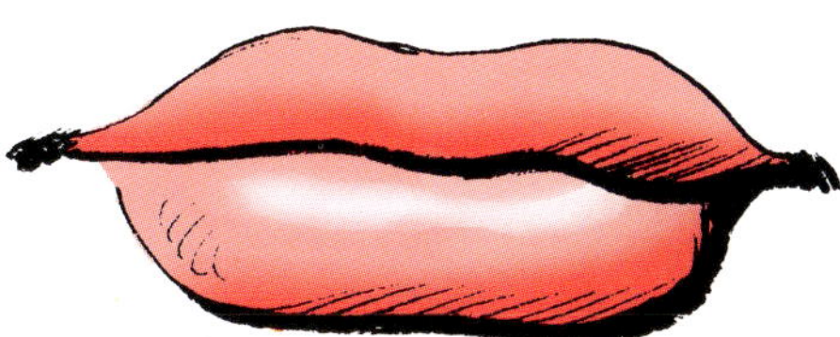

CHIN AND JAW
Firm and determined. Occasionally, the chin is dimpled or cleft.

LIPS
Full and pouty to give them a moody quality. The lower lip is always fuller than the upper lip.

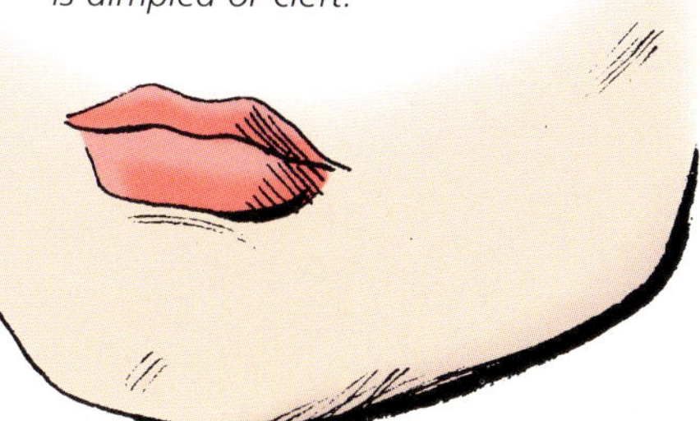

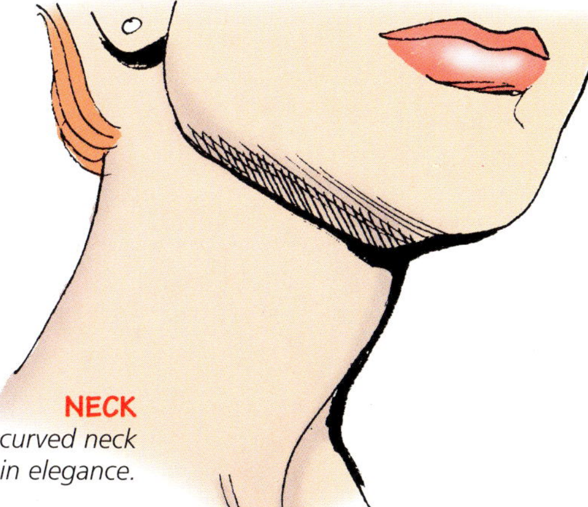

NECK
A long, gently curved neck suggests a certain elegance.

WOMEN'S COSTUMES

The typical female hero is tough, resourceful, and glamorous. She is self-reliant yet vulnerable. Sure, she can conquer a giant mutant, but she still carries with her the loneliness of the human condition. This is what makes for great drama. Think about what your character needs, wants, and thinks when designing her. Think of her attitude, her inner turmoil. Make it speak through her eyes and body language.

When you design a costume for her, make it exciting, revealing, and daring. In the parallel universe where the futuristic comic book wars take place, the women do not have an ounce of fat on them, and their costumes show all their body lines. They are defiant and tough, but always extremely attractive.

Costumes and faces should be created together. Putting a soft, sweet, wholesome face on top of a skin-tight, warrior costume just won't look right.

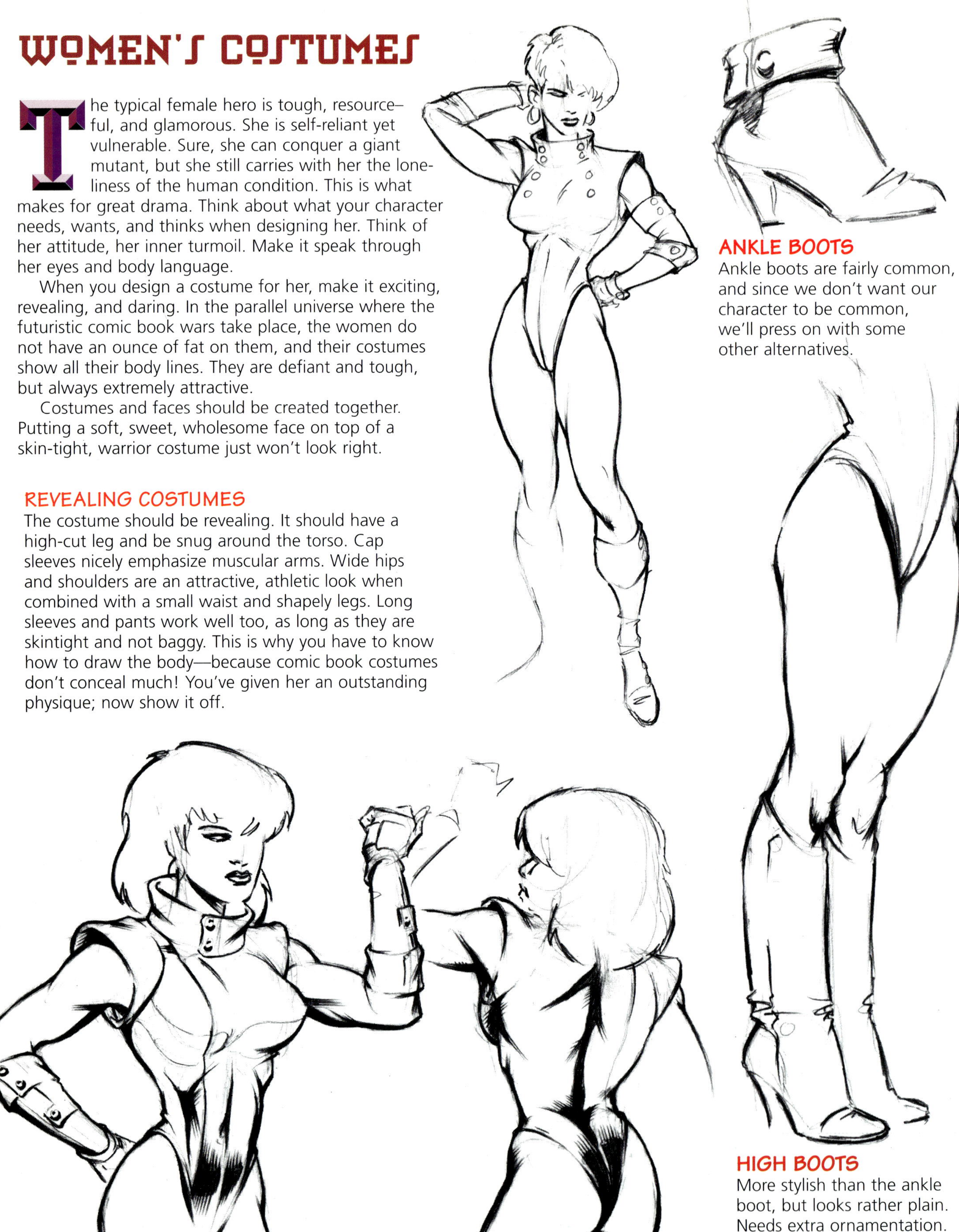

REVEALING COSTUMES

The costume should be revealing. It should have a high-cut leg and be snug around the torso. Cap sleeves nicely emphasize muscular arms. Wide hips and shoulders are an attractive, athletic look when combined with a small waist and shapely legs. Long sleeves and pants work well too, as long as they are skintight and not baggy. This is why you have to know how to draw the body—because comic book costumes don't conceal much! You've given her an outstanding physique; now show it off.

ANKLE BOOTS

Ankle boots are fairly common, and since we don't want our character to be common, we'll press on with some other alternatives.

HIGH BOOTS

More stylish than the ankle boot, but looks rather plain. Needs extra ornamentation.

DROP-DEAD GORGEOUS

The female action hero is constructed with an emphasis on athleticism. She should display a physique that looks as if she can take on the world, yet she should still maintain her feminine allure.

The legs should be slightly elongated, tapering at the ankle. Overly muscular legs tend to appear too heavy.

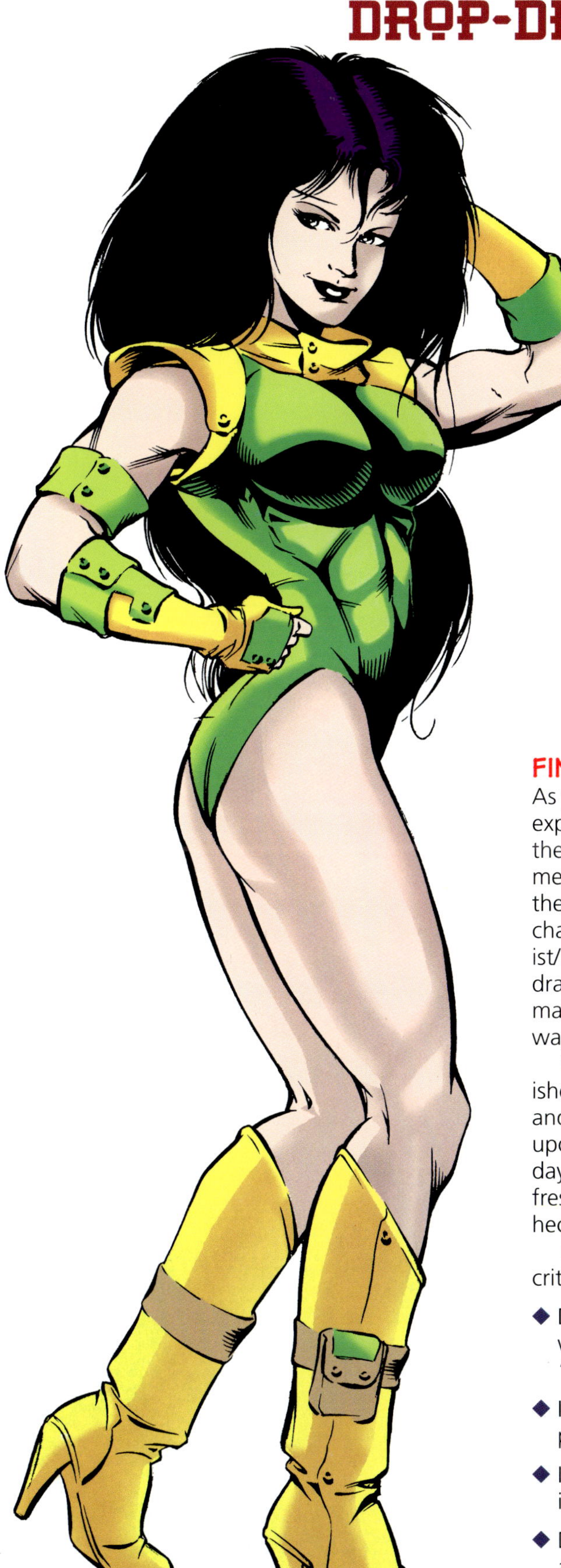

FINAL VERSION

As you now know, no one, not even an experienced comic book artist, hits it right the first time. It's trial and error. Experimentation. Beginners typically feel that their drawing is etched in stone, and resist changing it. But the professional cartoonist/illustrator doesn't regard any single drawing as precious, and he continues to make adjustments until he cannot see a way to improve it further.

When you feel that a drawing is finished, it's always a good idea to step back and take a look. How can you improve upon it? By reviewing a drawing the next day, you can usually approach it with a fresh perspective and really lacerate the heck out of it.

Here are some things to look for when critiquing your own work:

- Does the character look like it has weight, or does it appear to just "float" on the page?
- Is there a sweep or flow to the overall pose?
- Is there a clear attitude that the drawing conveys?
- Does the character look flat, or does it appear round and lifelike?

TEEN HERO COSTUME

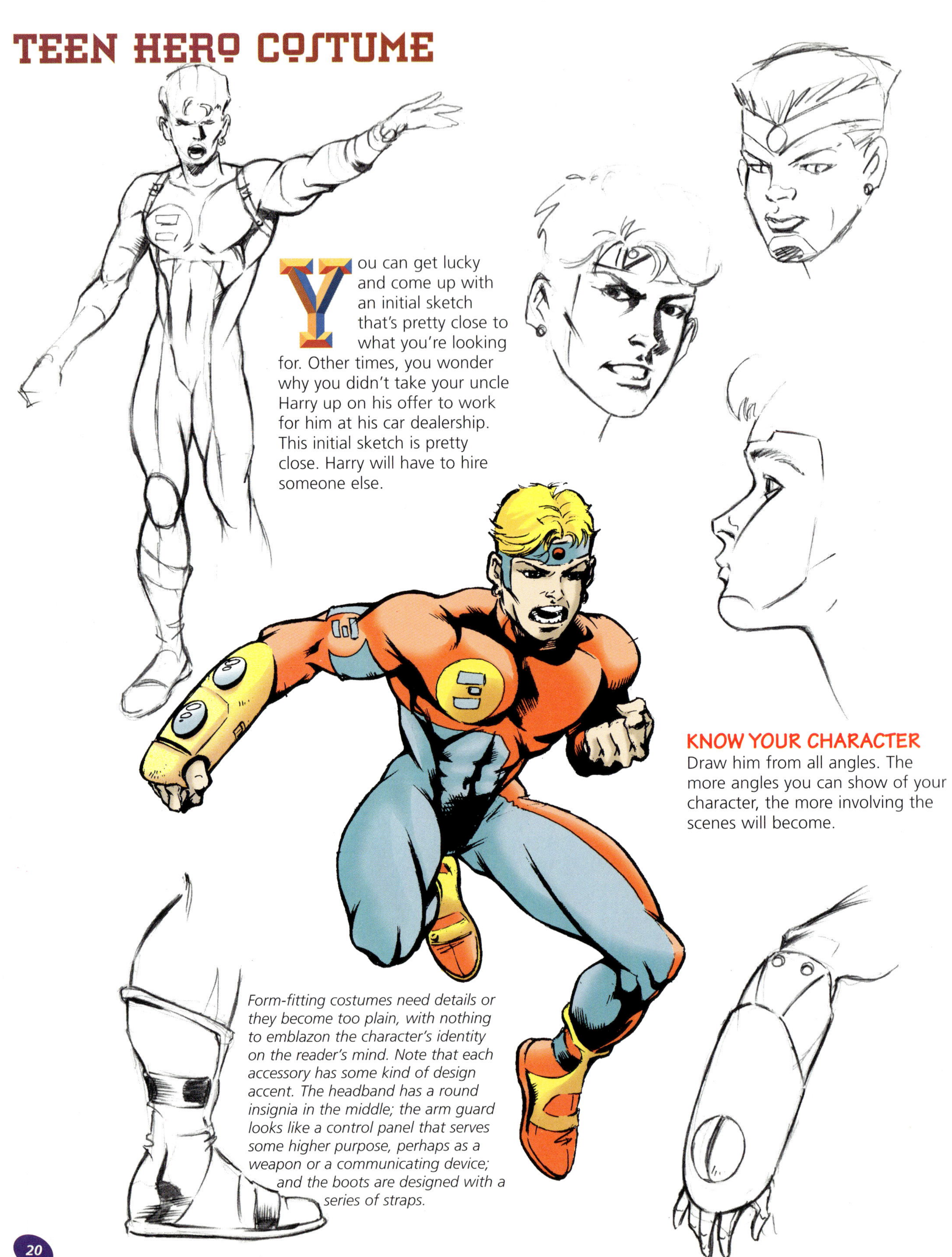

You can get lucky and come up with an initial sketch that's pretty close to what you're looking for. Other times, you wonder why you didn't take your uncle Harry up on his offer to work for him at his car dealership. This initial sketch is pretty close. Harry will have to hire someone else.

KNOW YOUR CHARACTER

Draw him from all angles. The more angles you can show of your character, the more involving the scenes will become.

Form-fitting costumes need details or they become too plain, with nothing to emblazon the character's identity on the reader's mind. Note that each accessory has some kind of design accent. The headband has a round insignia in the middle; the arm guard looks like a control panel that serves some higher purpose, perhaps as a weapon or a communicating device; and the boots are designed with a series of straps.

WORLD'S BEST FLYING POSES

Do not be content to have your flying hero stick his hands in the air and start to soar. The thing that makes a flying pose dramatic is not so much that your character is airborne, but the way you depict the character *approaching* the reader or *receding* from the reader. These poses don't look flat. Each is coming at you or going away from you at an extreme angle. And the legs are not stuck together; they are just as carefully positioned as the arms. Whether the hands are open or closed, whether the pose has two arms out, one, or none, the foreshortening on the character must be *extreme*. You must make the part of the body that is nearer to the reader much larger than the part that is farther away.

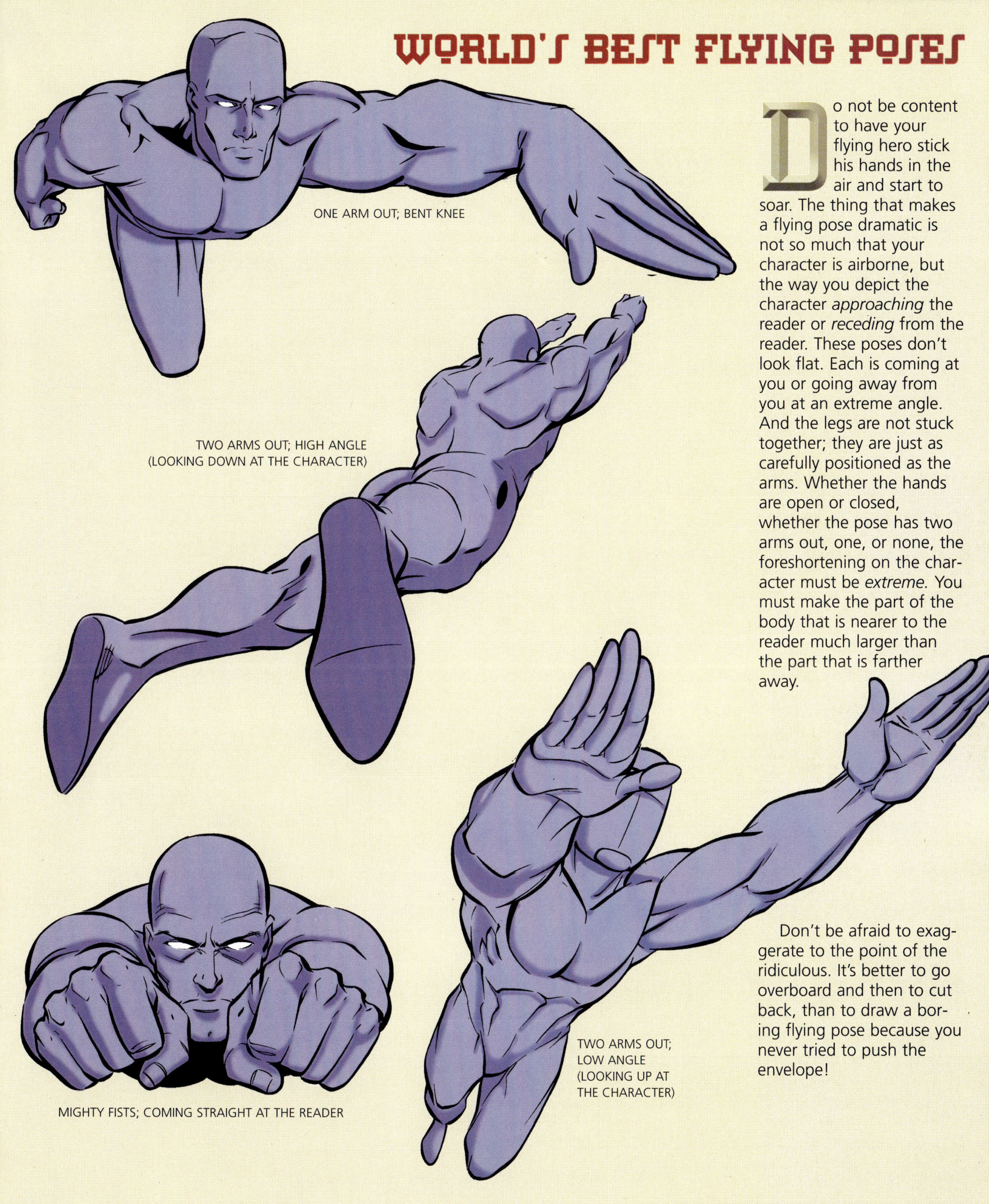

ONE ARM OUT; BENT KNEE

TWO ARMS OUT; HIGH ANGLE (LOOKING DOWN AT THE CHARACTER)

MIGHTY FISTS; COMING STRAIGHT AT THE READER

TWO ARMS OUT; LOW ANGLE (LOOKING UP AT THE CHARACTER)

Don't be afraid to exaggerate to the point of the ridiculous. It's better to go overboard and then to cut back, than to draw a boring flying pose because you never tried to push the envelope!

HOW TO DRAW THE CAPE

The cape has puzzled artists since the beginning of time. If you look at prehistoric art painted on cave walls, you will see that none of the figures wear capes. It was just too difficult for Cro-Magnon man to draw.

Fast forward 50,000 years. True, we haven't solved the problems of hunger or war, but boy, can we draw great capes! Now this is the epitome of progress.

Unless you learn how to draw the folds in the cape, make it billow dramatically in the wind, and make it hang convincingly from the shoulders, your super hero is going to look like he's wearing a long napkin on his back. So pay attention. This section is for *you.*

THE HANGING CAPE—NORMAL

A cape hangs all the way to the feet, stopping just above the ground. When it hangs straight down, the cape has just a few folds that are long and sleek. Hey, if you ever bothered to make your bed, like your mom has been nagging you to do since you were nine, you'd know about folds by now. But since you didn't, I have to go into all of this. Sheesh! The cape drapes over the shoulders. The arms akimbo stance (fists on hips) is a classic for a caped character.

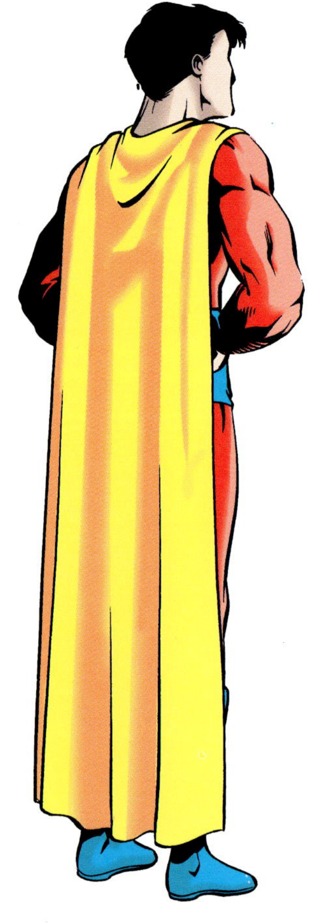

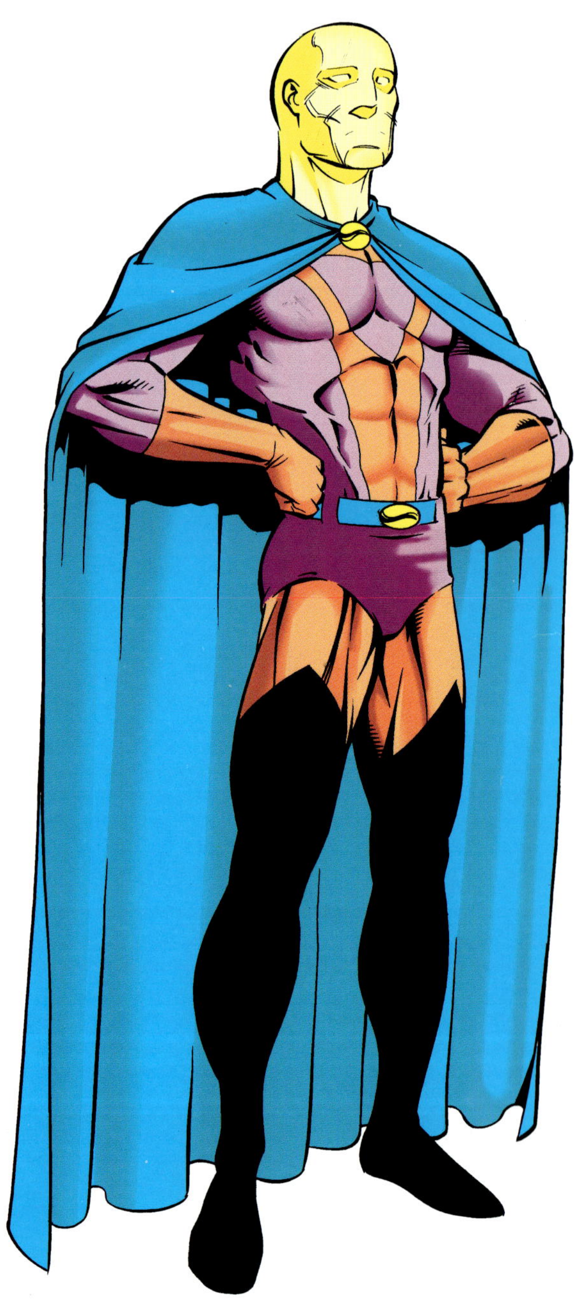

THE HANGING CAPE—WIDE

When a character wears a wide cape, the cape will drape over the arms, if the character stands in the classic arms-on-hips pose. The wider cape is somewhat more mysterious, but the dry cleaning bills are higher—so it's a trade off.

PROFESSIONAL HINT

This is important: By drawing one continuous line, you can more easily plot the folds, and then later erase the parts that are overlapped by the cape.

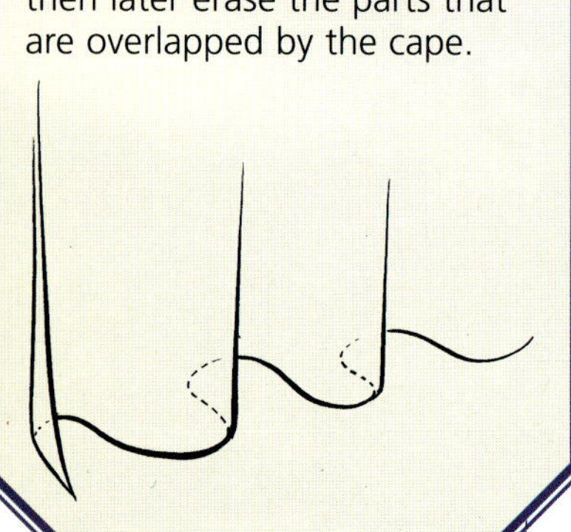

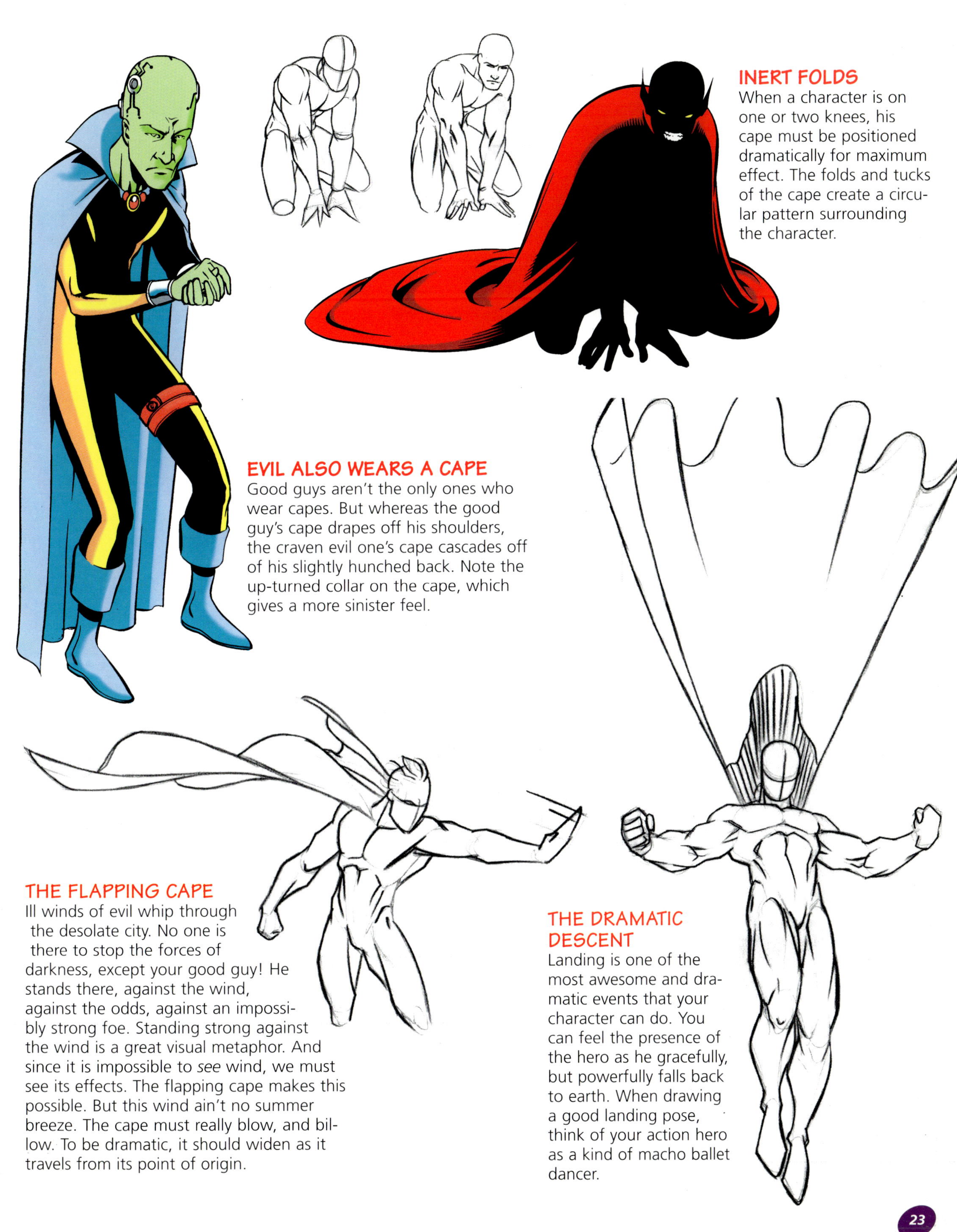

INERT FOLDS

When a character is on one or two knees, his cape must be positioned dramatically for maximum effect. The folds and tucks of the cape create a circular pattern surrounding the character.

EVIL ALSO WEARS A CAPE

Good guys aren't the only ones who wear capes. But whereas the good guy's cape drapes off his shoulders, the craven evil one's cape cascades off of his slightly hunched back. Note the up-turned collar on the cape, which gives a more sinister feel.

THE FLAPPING CAPE

Ill winds of evil whip through the desolate city. No one is there to stop the forces of darkness, except your good guy! He stands there, against the wind, against the odds, against an impossibly strong foe. Standing strong against the wind is a great visual metaphor. And since it is impossible to *see* wind, we must see its effects. The flapping cape makes this possible. But this wind ain't no summer breeze. The cape must really blow, and billow. To be dramatic, it should widen as it travels from its point of origin.

THE DRAMATIC DESCENT

Landing is one of the most awesome and dramatic events that your character can do. You can feel the presence of the hero as he gracefully, but powerfully falls back to earth. When drawing a good landing pose, think of your action hero as a kind of macho ballet dancer.

POPULAR COMIC BOOK GENRES

SWORD & SORCERY

There are many popular styles of comic book adventures for you to choose from. One such genre is "Sword and Sorcery," which was all but forgotten until the emergence of *Conan the Barbarian*. Now it's back with a vengeance. Taking place in a post-apocalyptic world, in prehistoric times, in other dimensions, far into the future, or on other planets, it is a perfect showcase for your innovations.

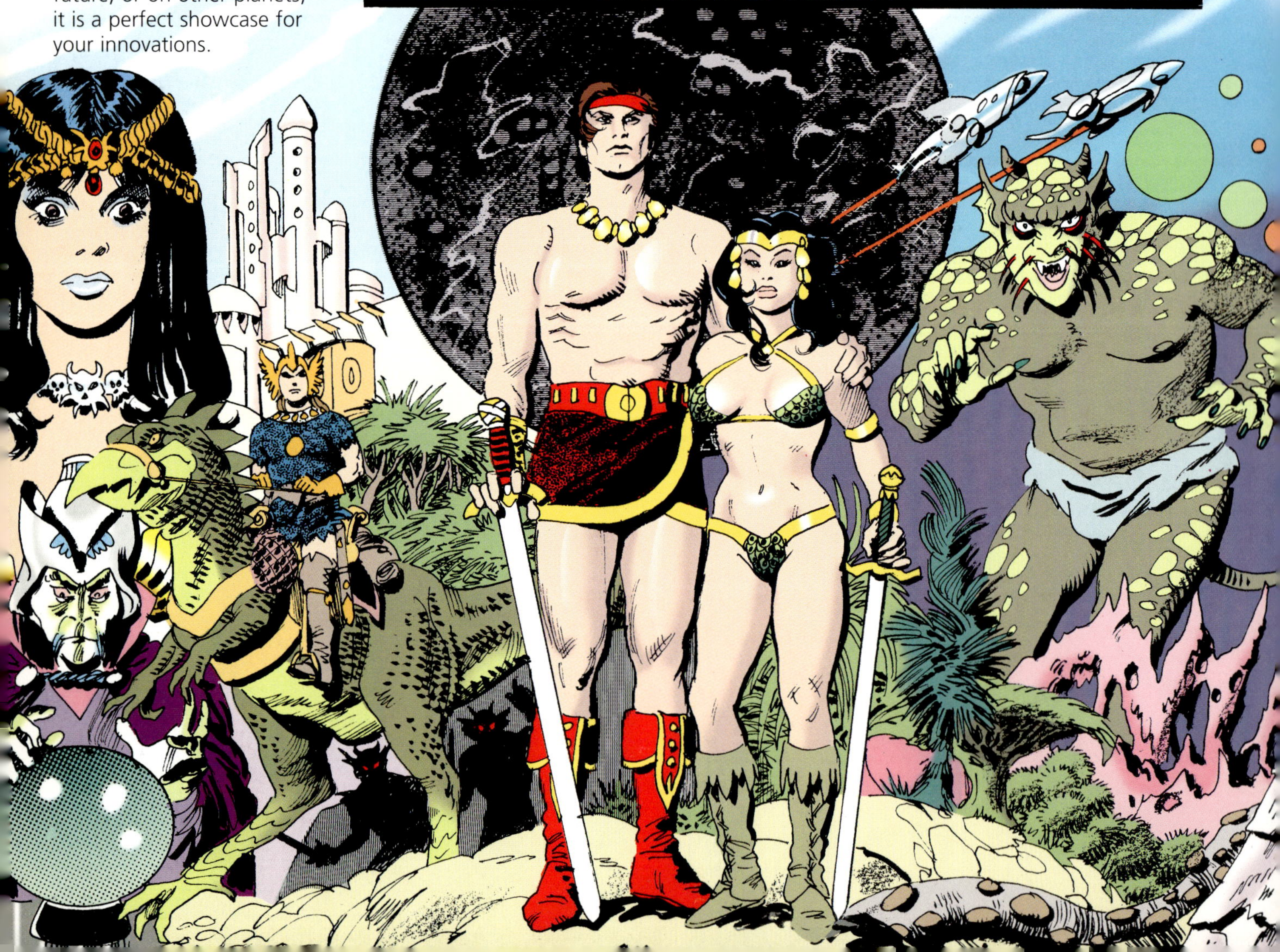

The heroes of these epics are not usually depicted as noble characters like Tarzan. They have hardened attitudes, usually evidenced by a scruffy beard and perhaps a few battle scars. They are gritty, grumpy, and blood-thirsty.

The women are among the most attractive in the comic book world. They give new meaning to the old adage, "The female of the species is deadlier than the male."

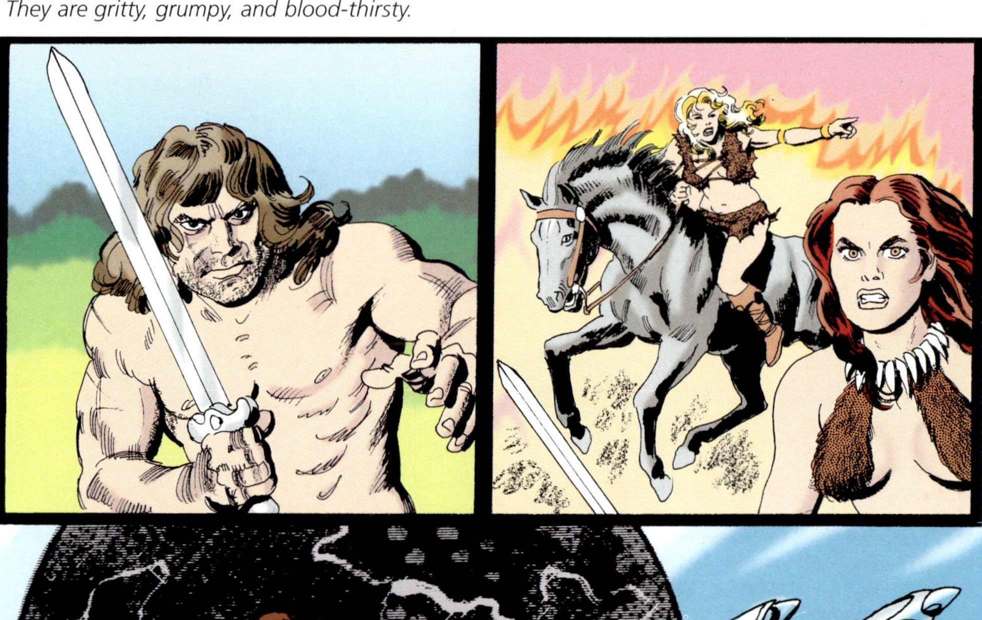

A SURREAL FOREST

Research real plant life or explore your 'fridge's vegetable tray, just twist it a bit.

WIZARDS, WARLOCKS, AND WITCHES

These three are a staple of the genre.

MONSTERS

You can start by drawing bugs—they already look weird—and just elaborate a little.

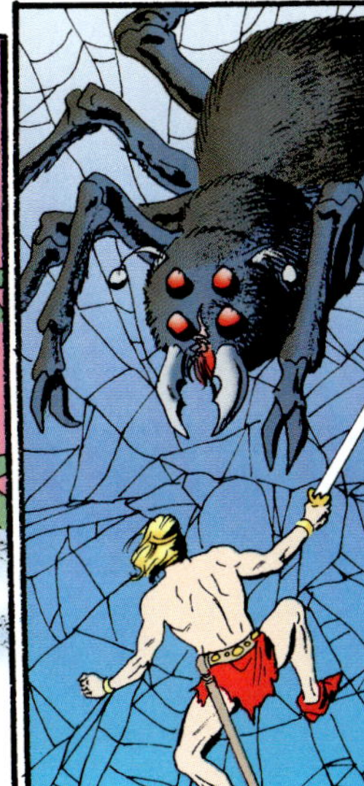

ROCK FORMATIONS

Think of how volcanoes and unusual weathering might have sculpted them.

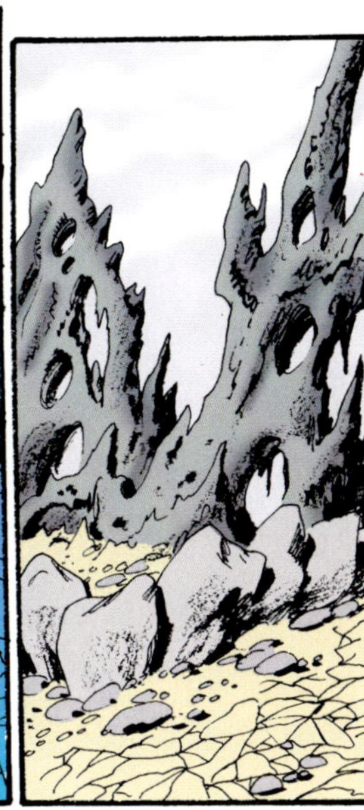

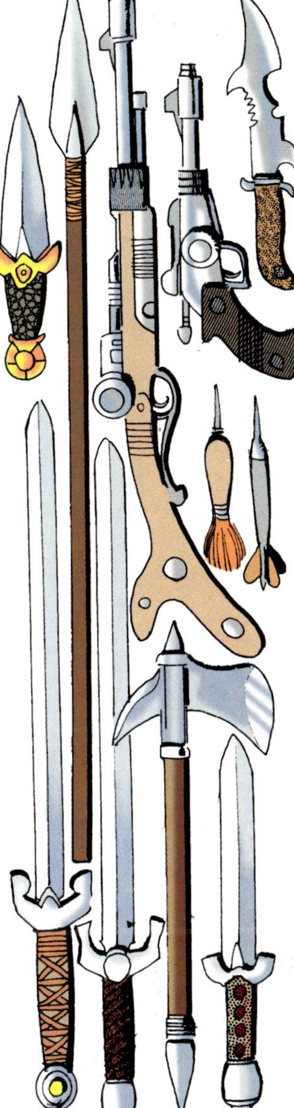

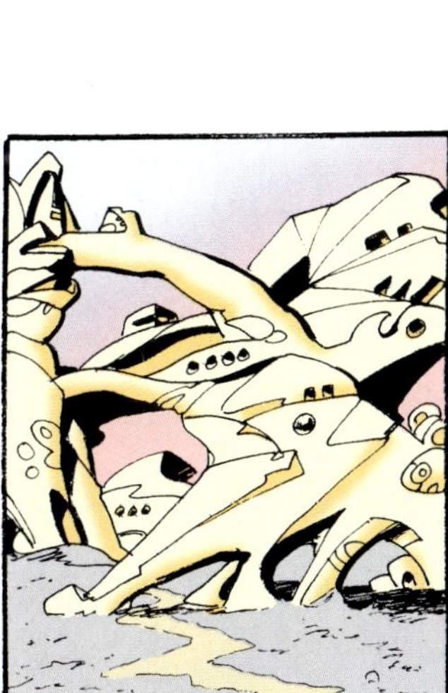

ARCHITECTURE

In reality, it's usually based on geometric shapes. So why not bend those shapes and create free-form constructions?

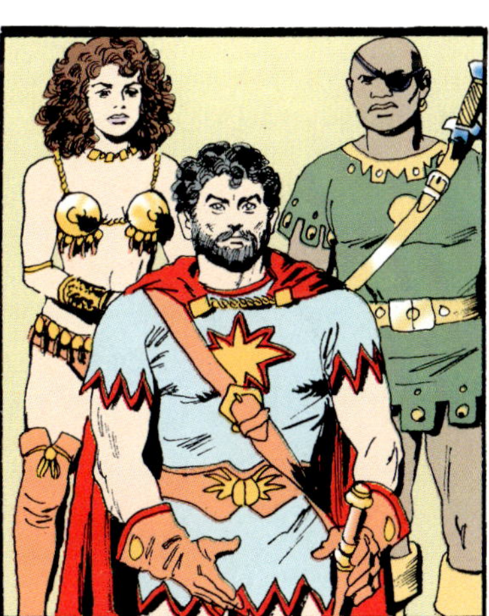

COSTUMING

Use anything you can conceive of that seems to suit. But keep in mind that sword and sorcery characters are burly, muscular folk, and the costumes should reflect that. Tailor the costumes to climate (i.e., temperate, desert, or arctic).

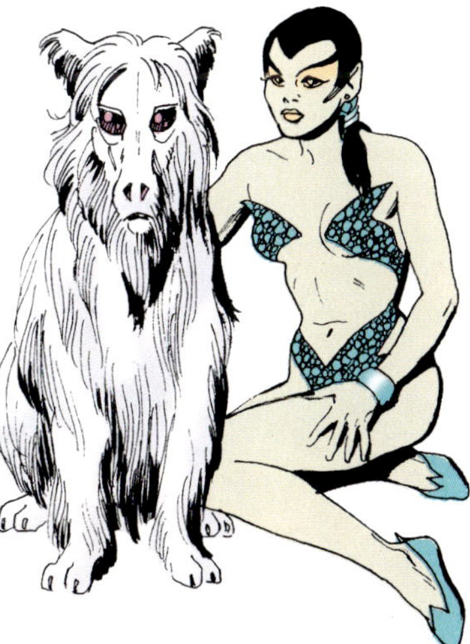

OTHER LIFE FORMS

Whether beasts of burden or marine life, wildlife or pets, it's fun to invent these creatures. It adds to the magical feeling of this fantasy genre.

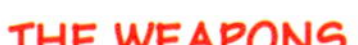

THE WEAPONS

You can visit your local library for more information on weapons—and check out material devoted to various fencing and fighting techniques. Try to impart the tension involved as the combatants attempt to slice, dice, and puncture each other with cold steel; a consideration sufficient to cause the knees to get weak in all but the hardiest of adversaries. Swords, hatchets, stilettos, darts, spears, and scimitars all appear in the sword and sorcery genre, and, occasionally, sci-fi weapons such as ray-guns and the like. Many of these weapons are heavy, so keep in mind that they are swung with big, dramatic motions.

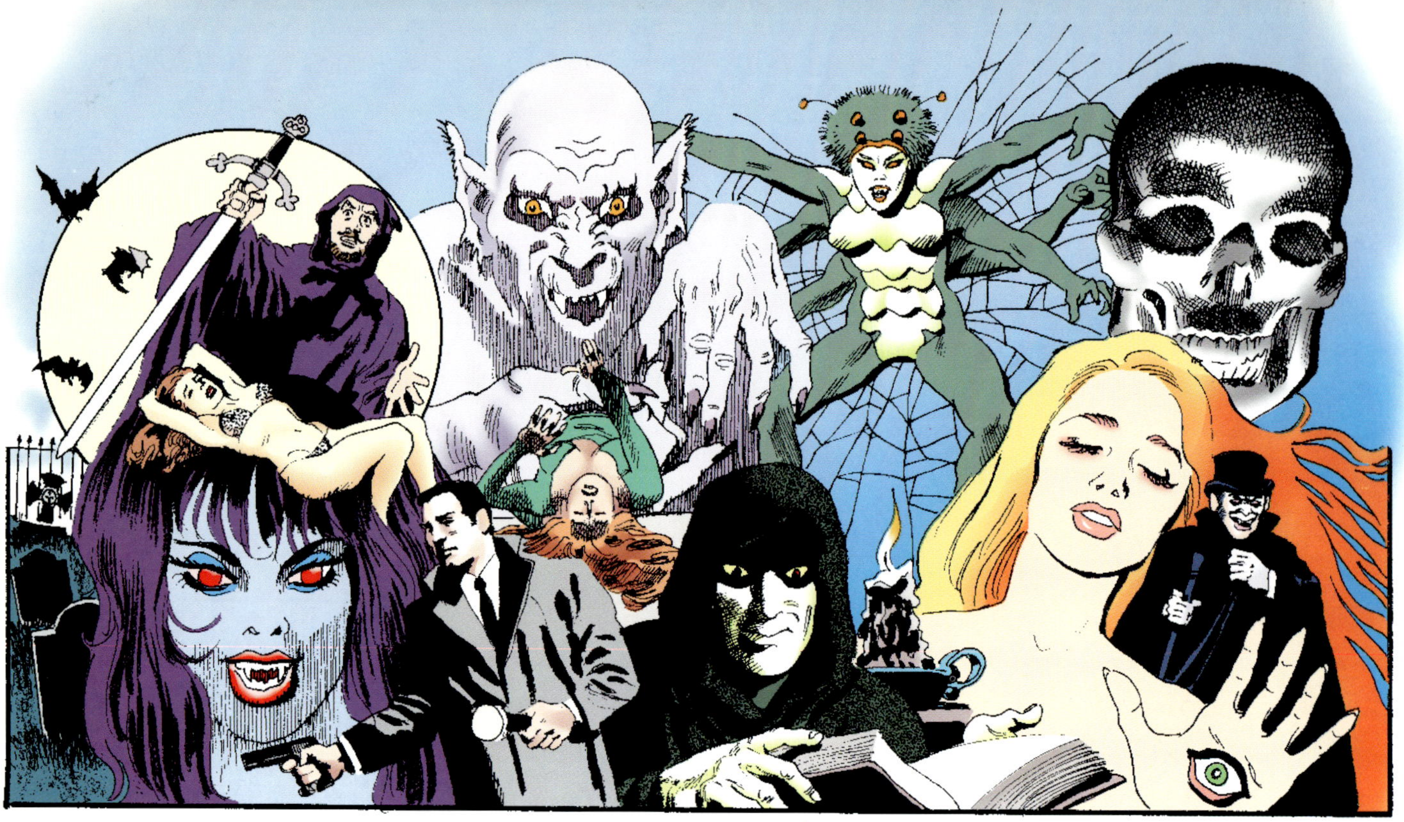

HORROR These are the things that go bump in the night. It's fun to be scared, as long as it's not serious. Ghouls, beasts, vampires, skeletons, giant insects, evil spirits, bats, and zombies all appeal to the dark, shadowy side of our imaginations. Horror often capitalizes on gothic themes of good versus evil, with man's fragile morality caught in the middle.

MILITARY With everything so technologically advanced these days, it can actually be *more* dramatic to go back in time to World War I or World War II, when airplanes engaged in dogfights, where the heroes had no super-human powers—only their wits and lion-sized, patriotic hearts with which to conquer the bad guys. It's still an excellent setting for drama; after all, the entire free world was at stake!

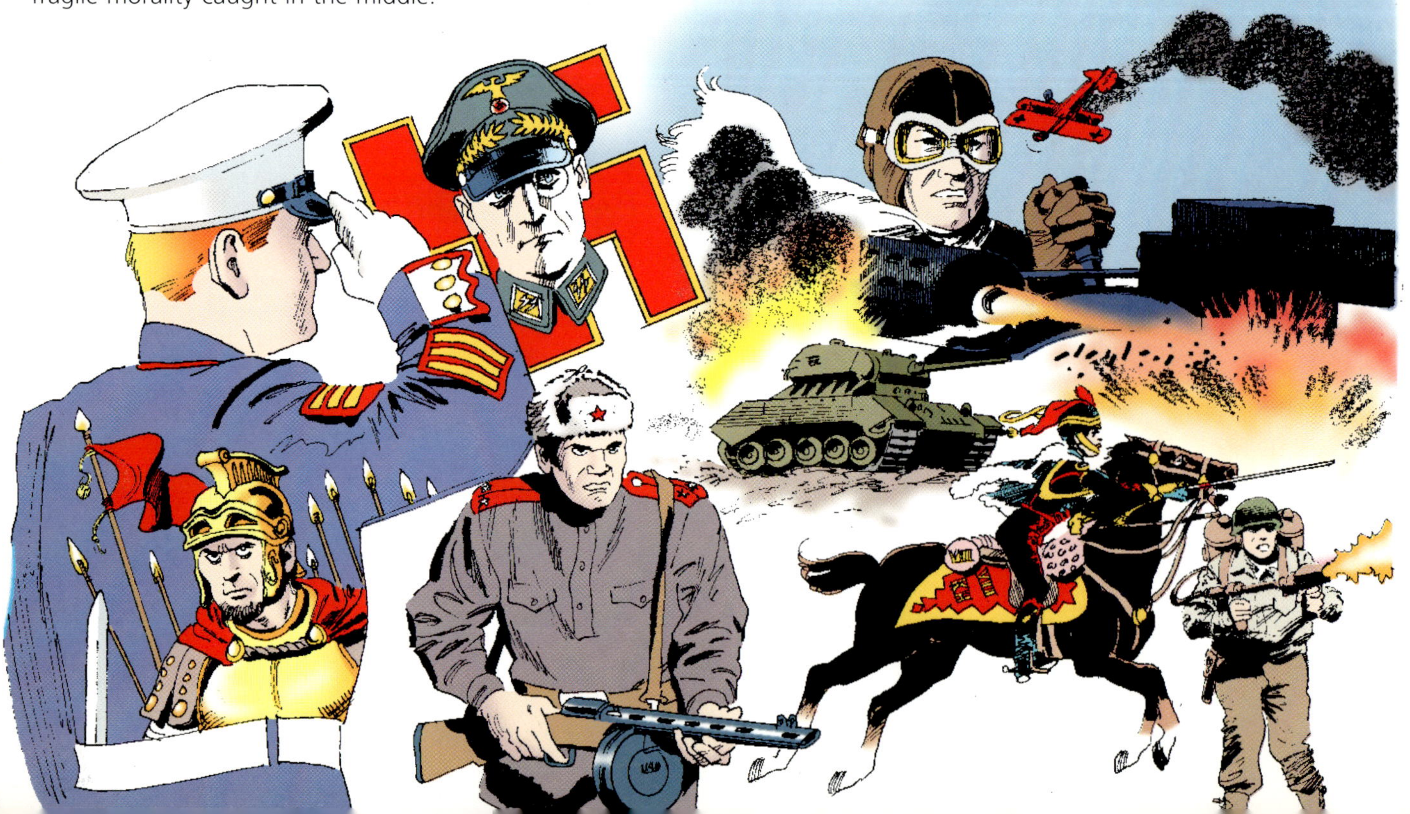

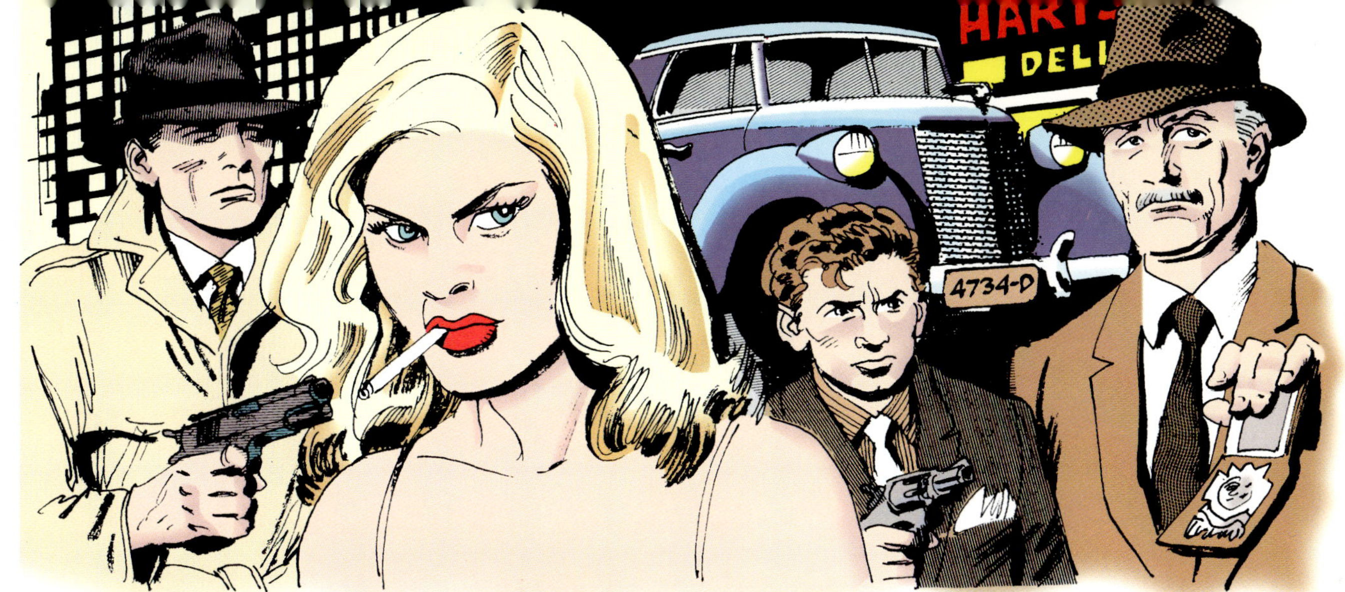

Detective Mysteries

Loyal fans gravitate to the terse words, thick atmosphere, and cynical characters that swirl around the plot of a detective story. The characters are hard-boiled, including the women—*especially* the women! They must be street-wise or they don't last long. Murder is always close behind, and money is out in front. Can romance exist in this distrustful and dangerous environment? You bet. But not the kind of romance that has picnics and walks along the beach. More like a black widow spider and her mate in a ritual dance of death.

WESTERNS AND BEYOND

New life has been infused into this genre by combining it with other genres, like the horror/western, the sci-fi/western, the contemporary western, the spy/western, and of course, the romance/western.

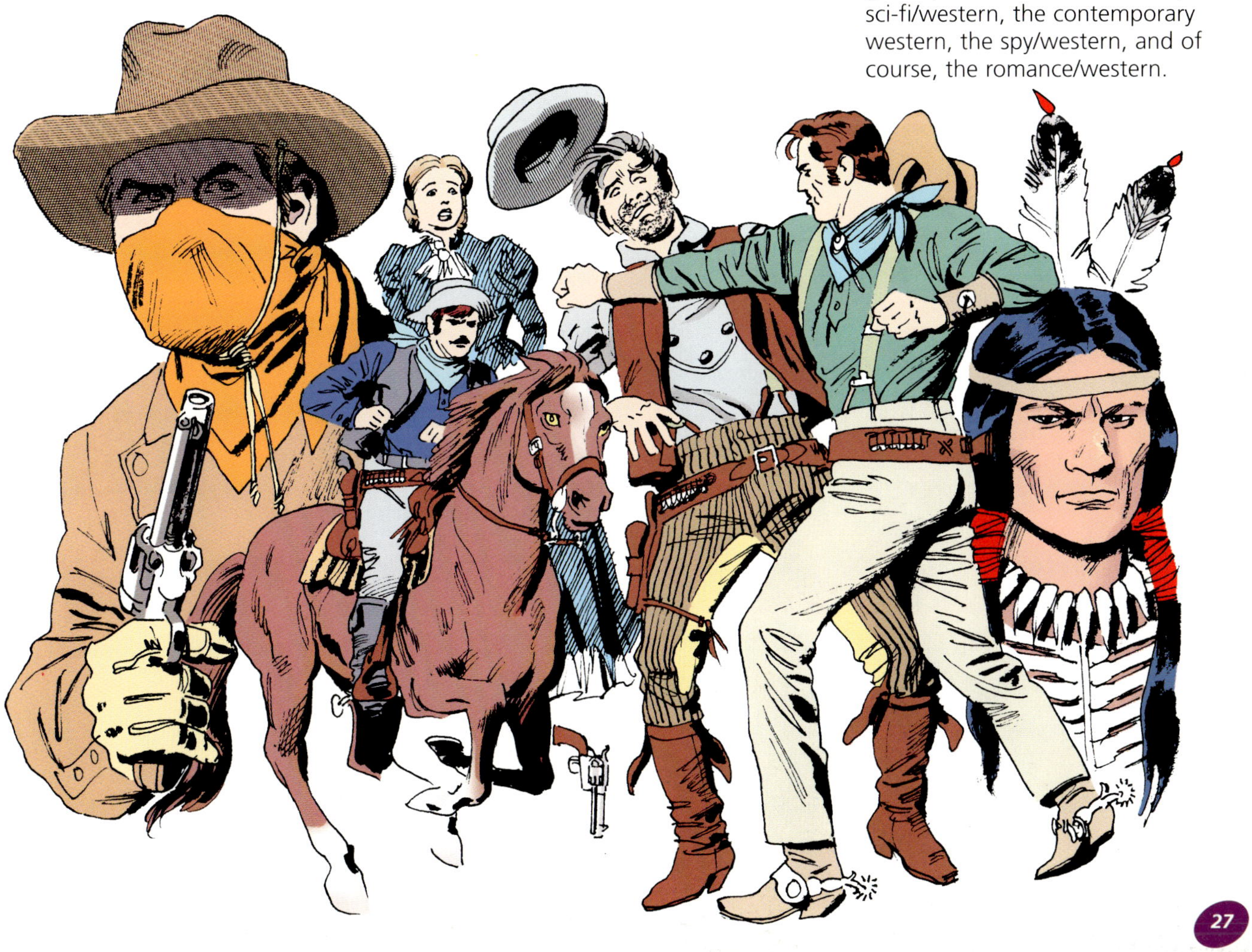

HASTA LA VISTA, BABY!

This is the real heavy metal, and I'm not talking about music. I'm talking artillery. You've got a big hero character? Give him a big gun. He'll need it, because his enemy is even more powerful. These guns take two hands to hold.

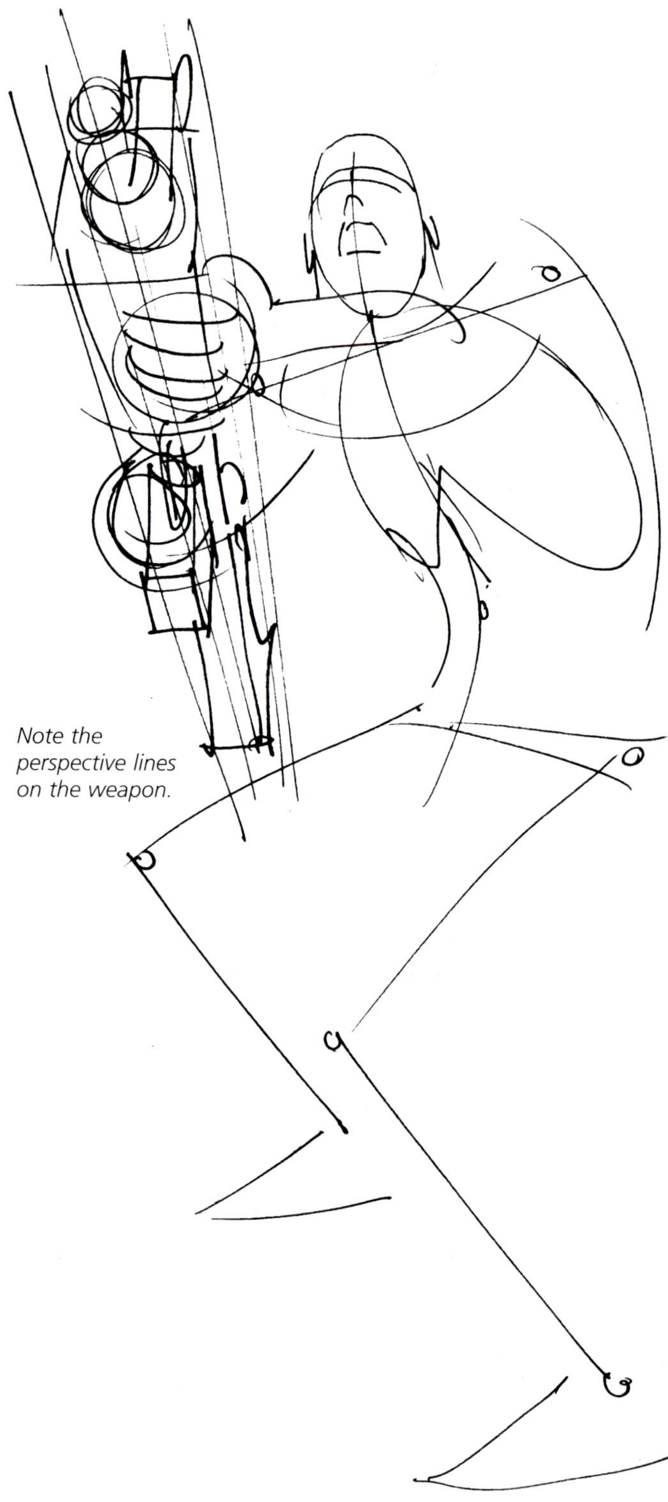

Note the perspective lines on the weapon.

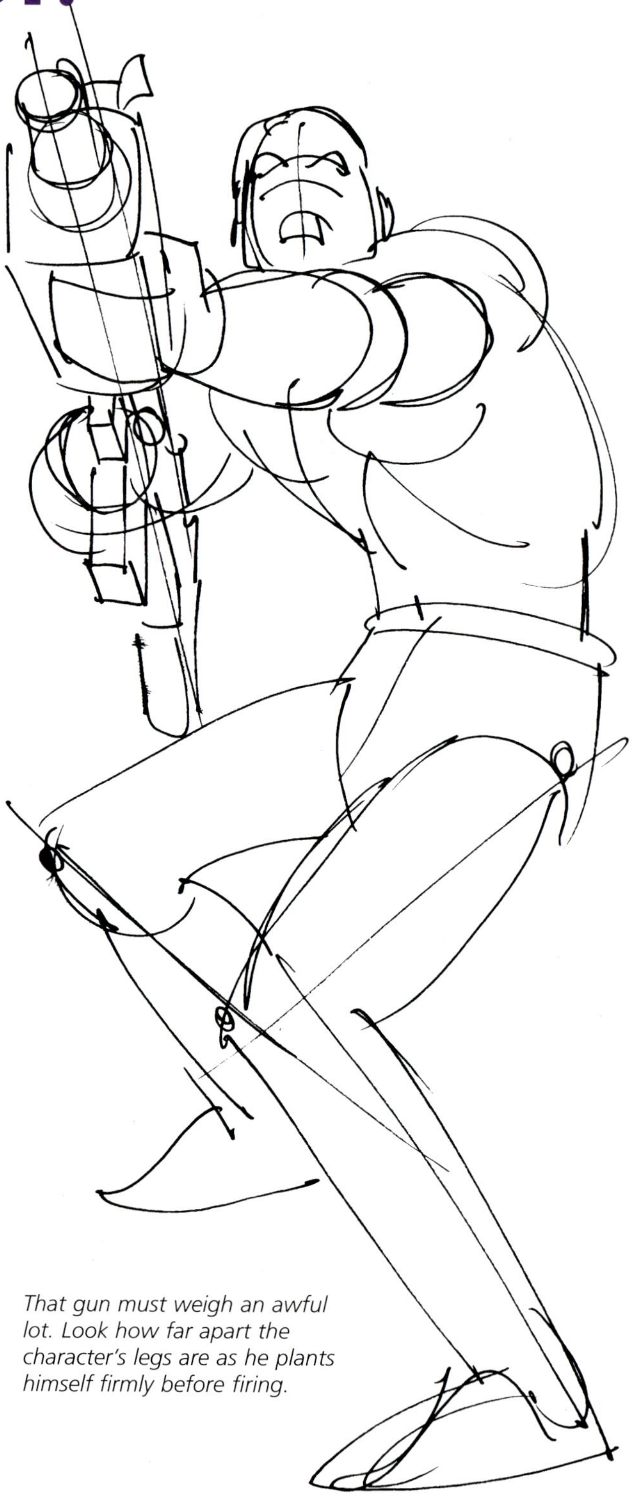

That gun must weigh an awful lot. Look how far apart the character's legs are as he plants himself firmly before firing.

STRAIGHT ARM POSE

A gun held away from the body can be a very dramatic pose. In this pose, the gunman can spray an area with bullets.

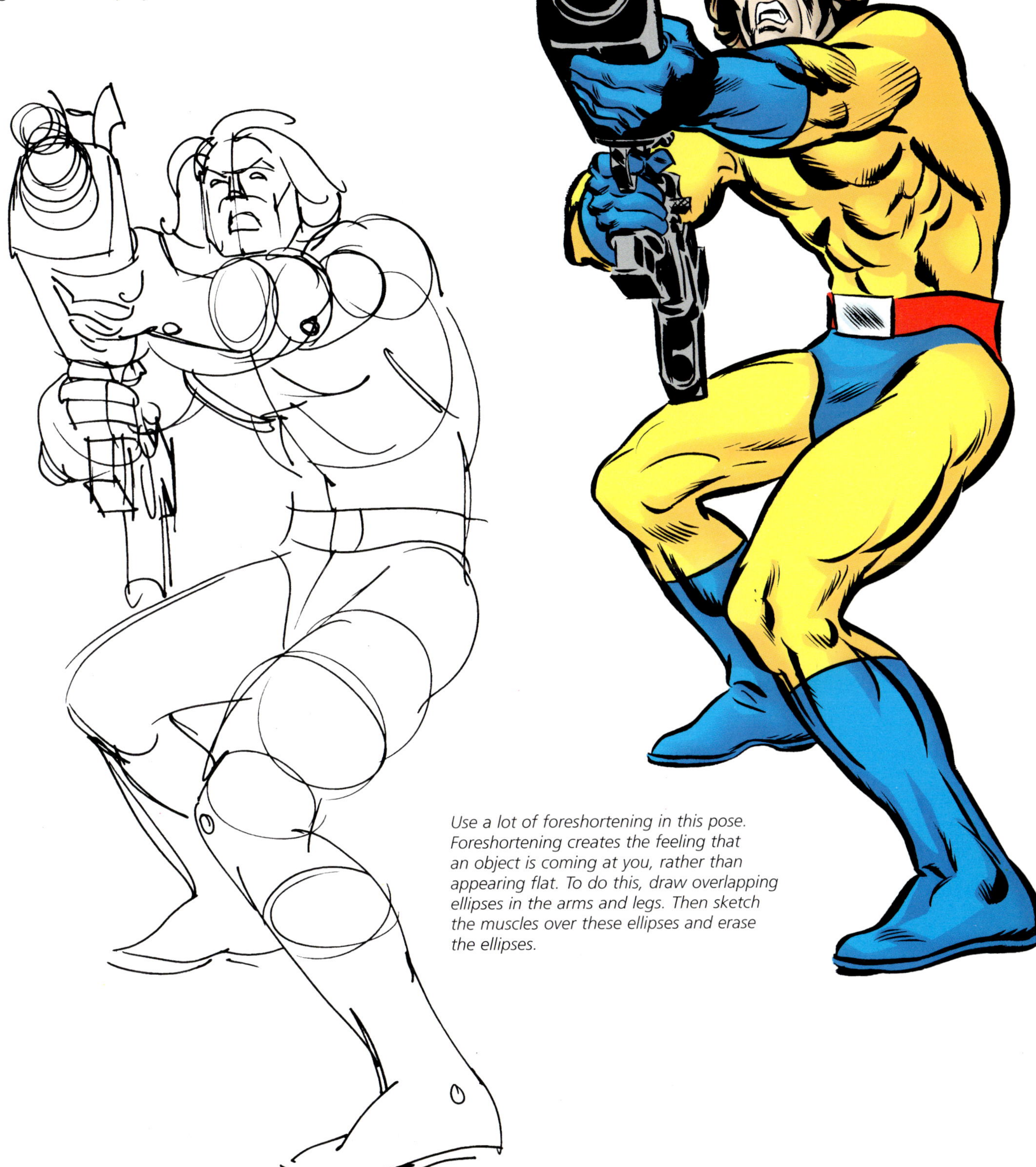

Use a lot of foreshortening in this pose. Foreshortening creates the feeling that an object is coming at you, rather than appearing flat. To do this, draw overlapping ellipses in the arms and legs. Then sketch the muscles over these ellipses and erase the ellipses.

SHORT GRIP POSE

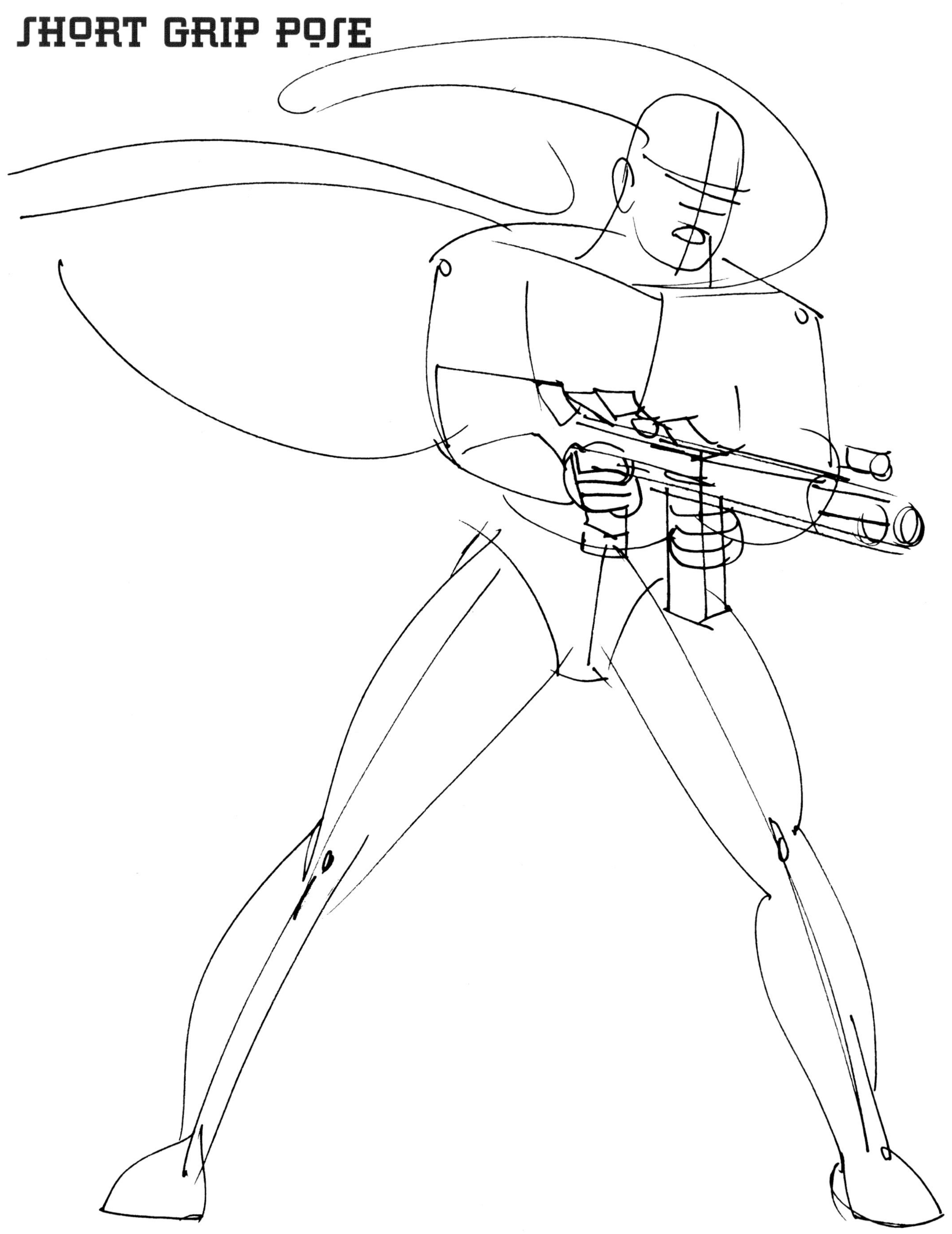

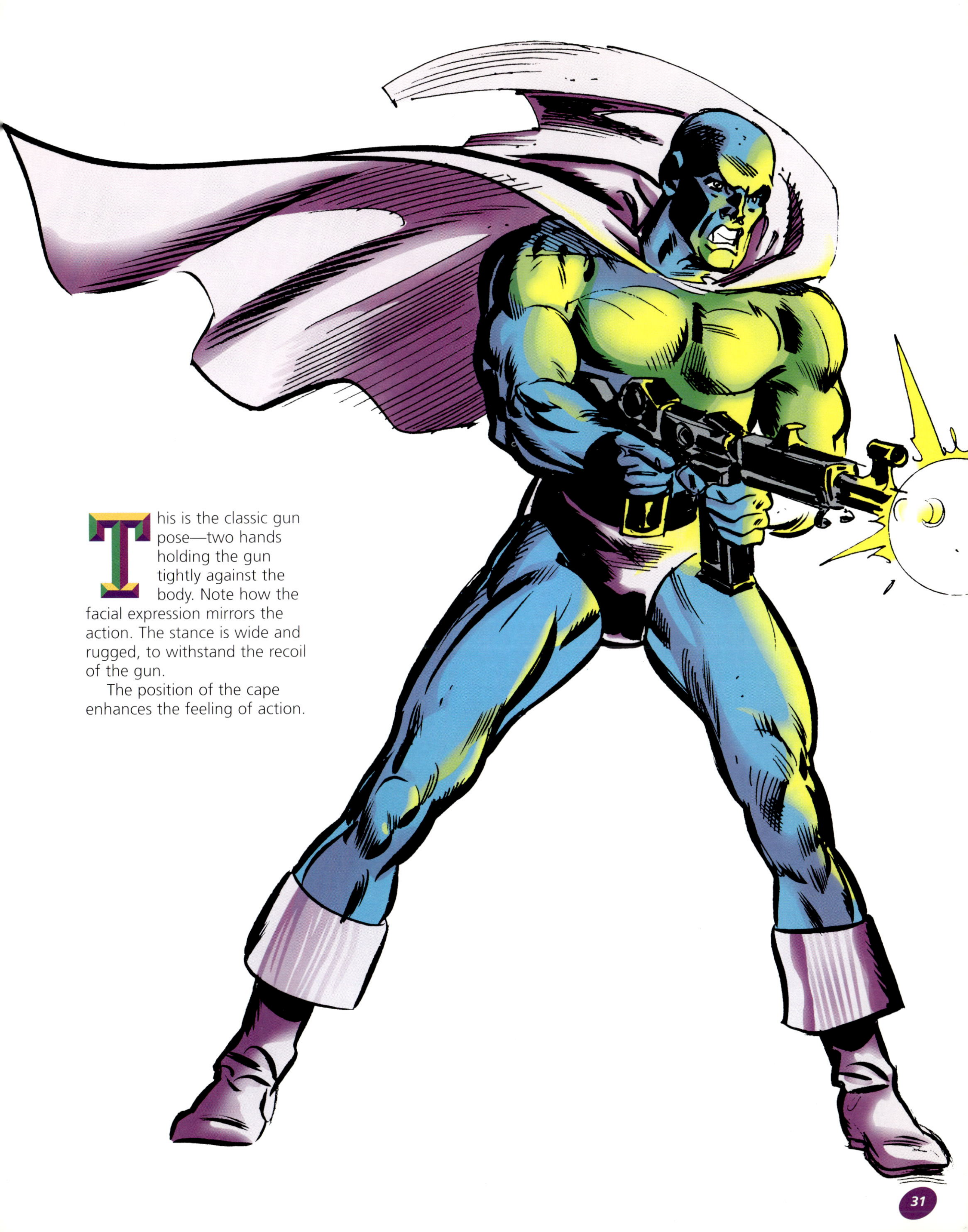

This is the classic gun pose—two hands holding the gun tightly against the body. Note how the facial expression mirrors the action. The stance is wide and rugged, to withstand the recoil of the gun.

The position of the cape enhances the feeling of action.

ROMANTIC MOMENTS

Comics are more than just Pow, Smash, Crunch, and Thud. There are tender moments that serve to add pacing to the hostile, battle-weary world that your heroes inhabit. A romantic moment also brings out the humanity in your characters and builds strong bonds between characters.

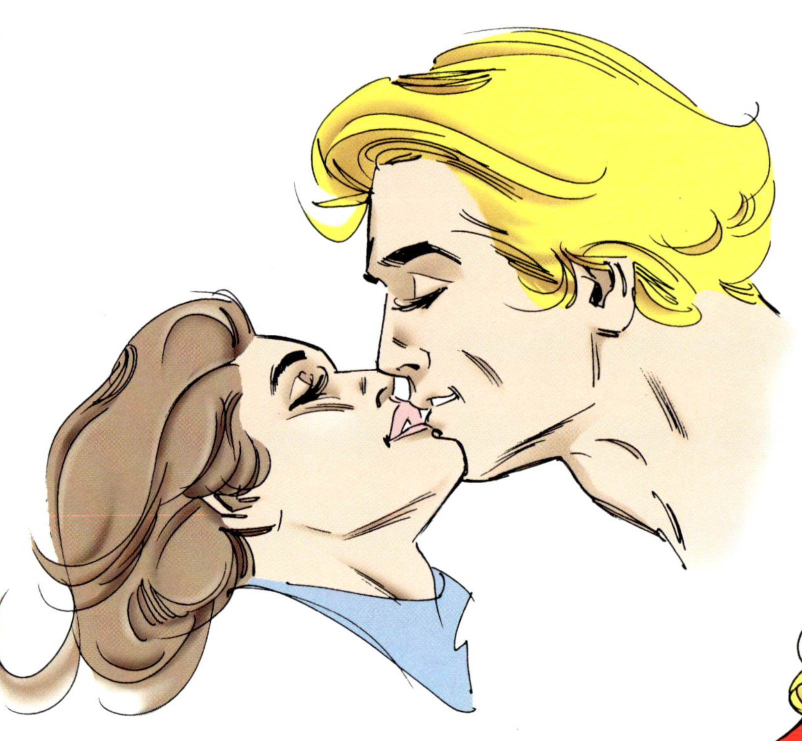

THE KISS

Notice how the faces angle in position to kiss. The noses overlap on one side while the chins overlap on the other side. The eyes are closed and the teeth show through slightly opened mouths.

THE TORRID EMBRACE

Arms should wrap around each other. Clinging to each other as if the world had disappeared. Look at the intensity in both characters' eyes. The man leans forward, the woman leans back. And the rest, as they say, is history.

ACTION-PACKED ROMANTIC MOMENTS

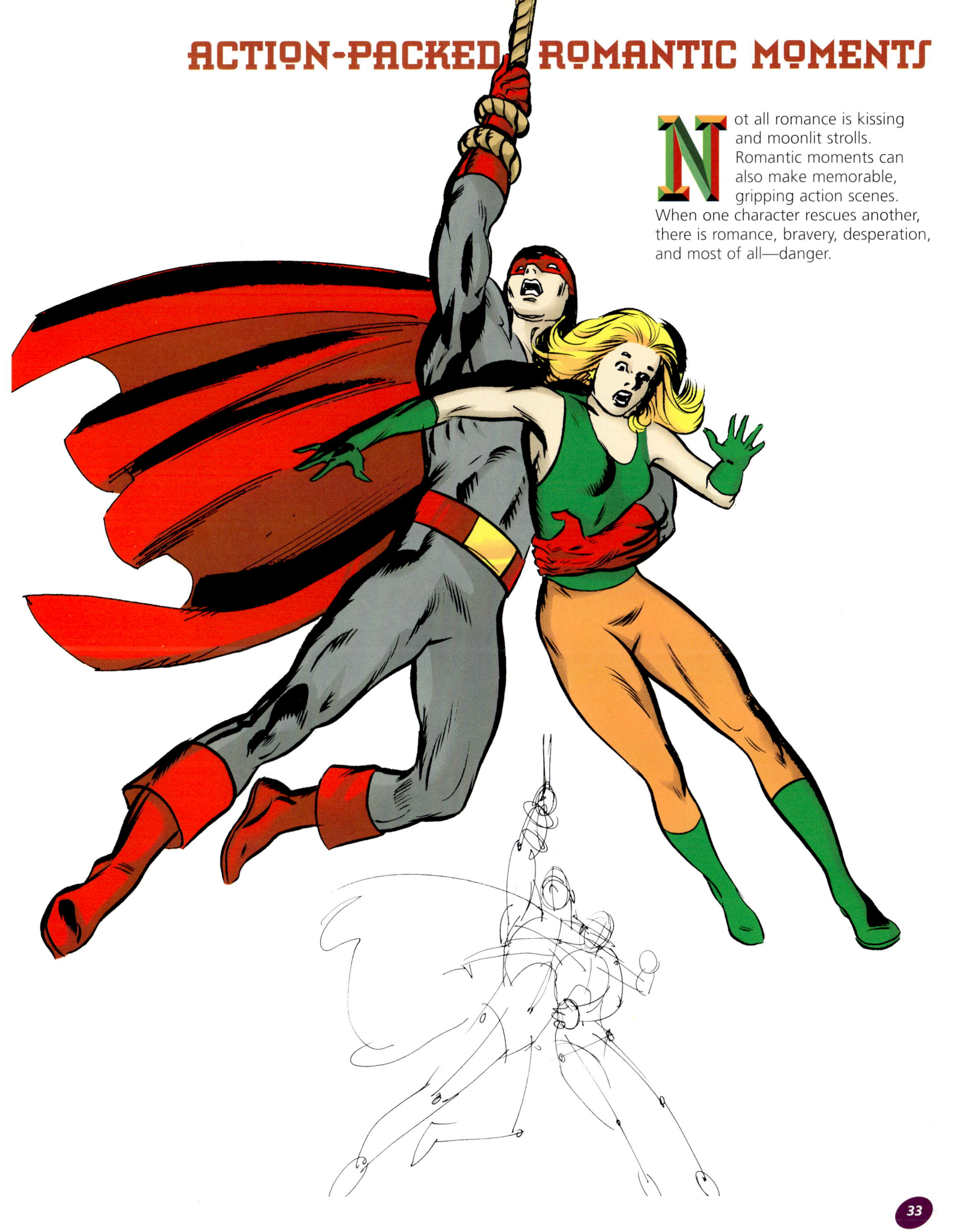

Not all romance is kissing and moonlit strolls. Romantic moments can also make memorable, gripping action scenes. When one character rescues another, there is romance, bravery, desperation, and most of all—danger.

PROFESSIONAL TRADE SECRETS

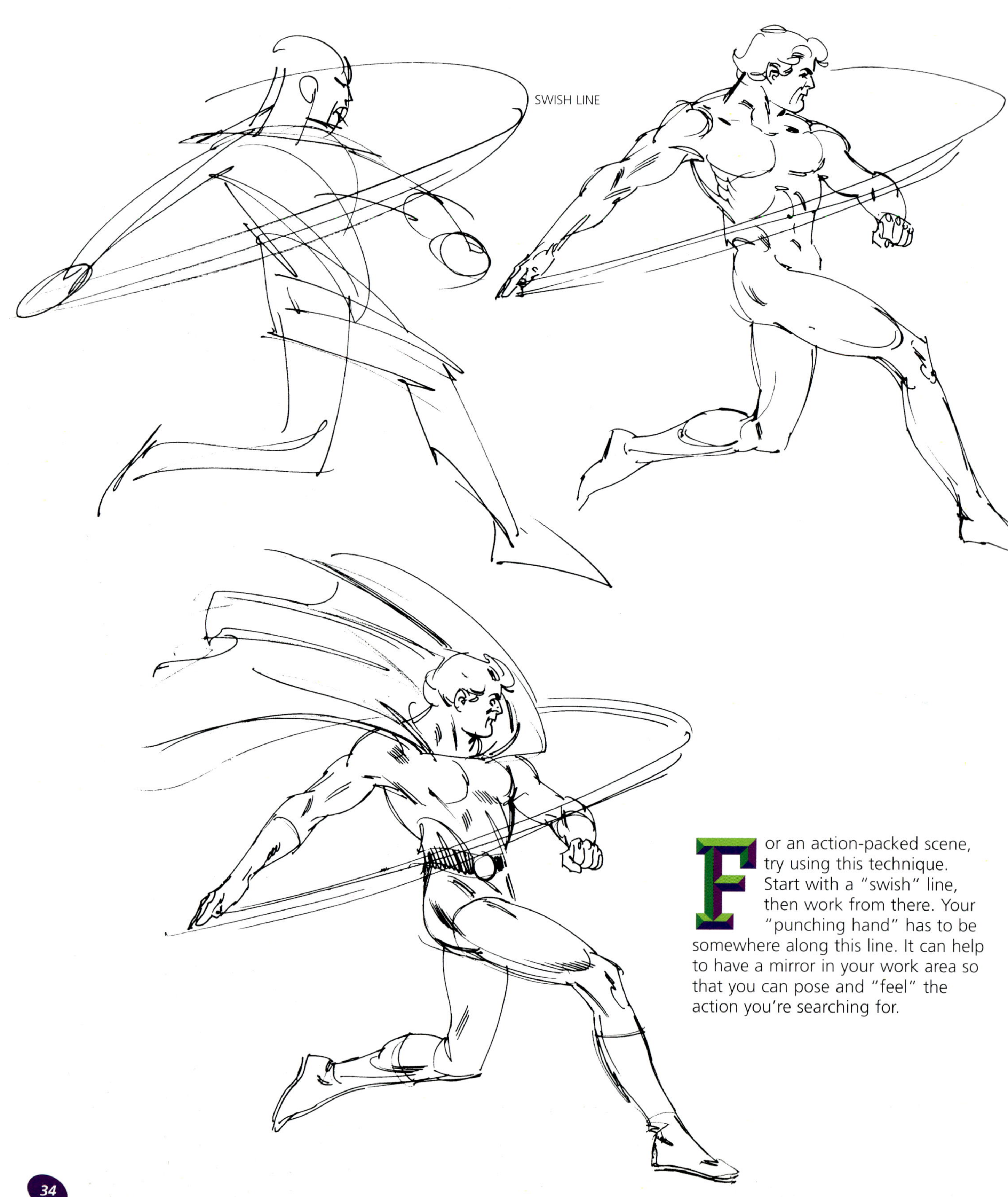

For an action-packed scene, try using this technique. Start with a "swish" line, then work from there. Your "punching hand" has to be somewhere along this line. It can help to have a mirror in your work area so that you can pose and "feel" the action you're searching for.

CREATING DRAMATIC IMAGES

What makes a dramatic image? What makes a boring image? What makes a great sandwich? I'll reveal the answers to the first two questions, but the sandwich secret dies with me. Sorry.

High and low angles, edge-lighting, under-lighting, mood, bursts, silhouettes, close-ups, and partial face close-ups are only some of the ways the pros turn good drawings into powerful images.

SINGLE AND DOUBLE SOURCES OF LIGHT *on a subject add interest to a scene. Note that the characters are not evenly bathed in light, rather, light is coming at the characters from particular directions, creating shadows.*

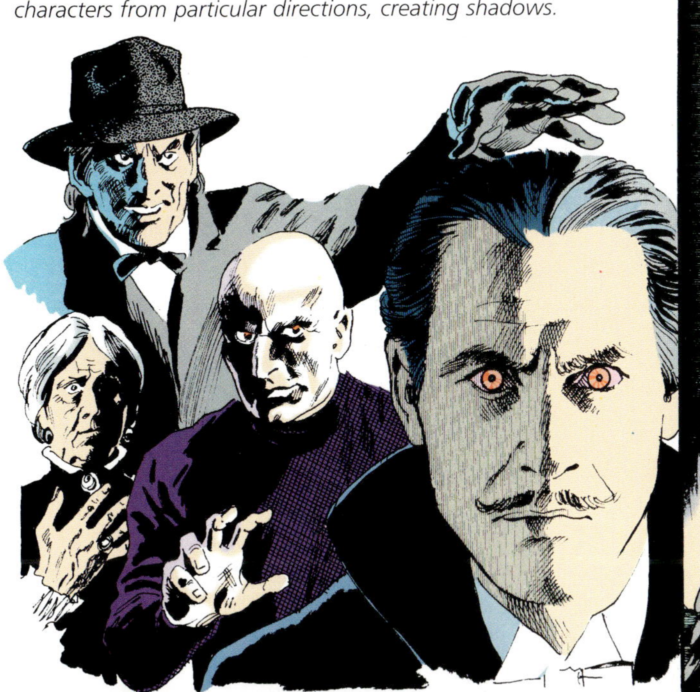

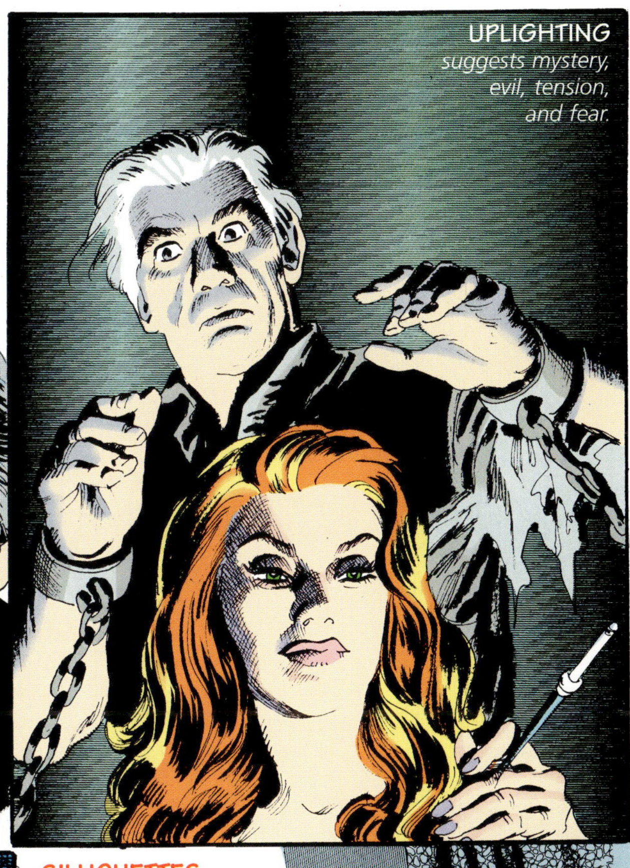

UPLIGHTING *suggests mystery, evil, tension, and fear.*

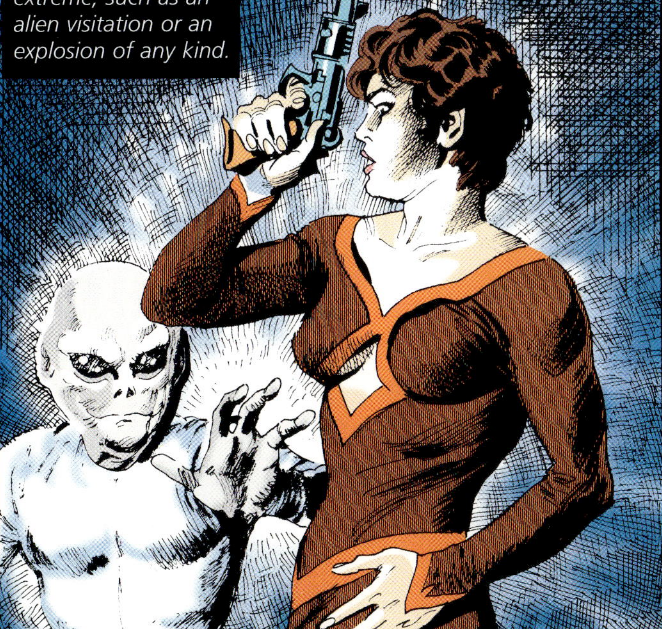

BURSTS *suggest something extreme, such as an alien visitation or an explosion of any kind.*

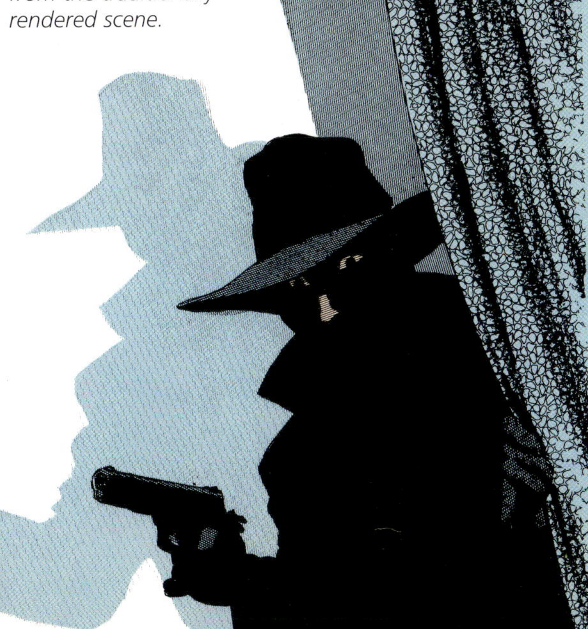

SILHOUETTES *suggest mystery or perhaps just a relief from the traditionally rendered scene.*

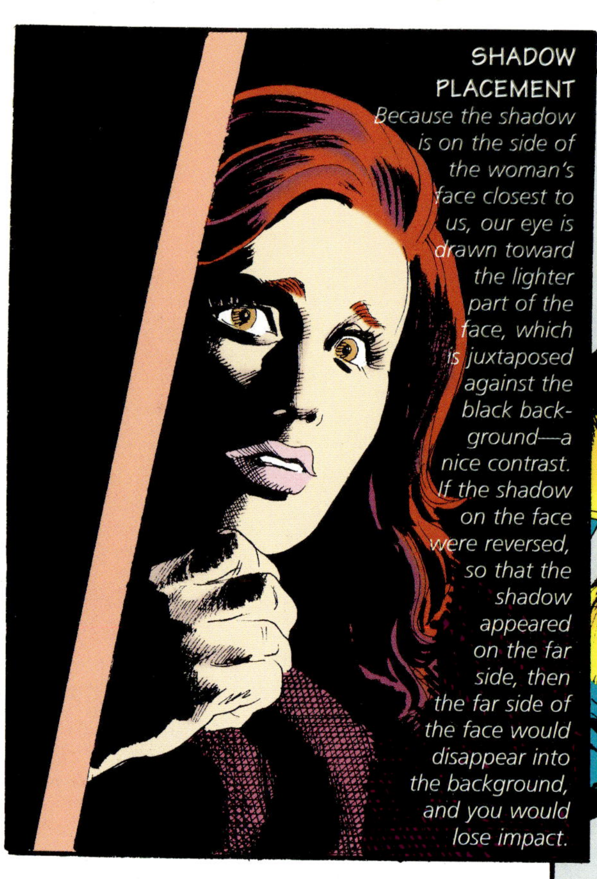

SHADOW PLACEMENT *Because the shadow is on the side of the woman's face closest to us, our eye is drawn toward the lighter part of the face, which is juxtaposed against the black background—a nice contrast. If the shadow on the face were reversed, so that the shadow appeared on the far side, then the far side of the face would disappear into the background, and you would lose impact.*

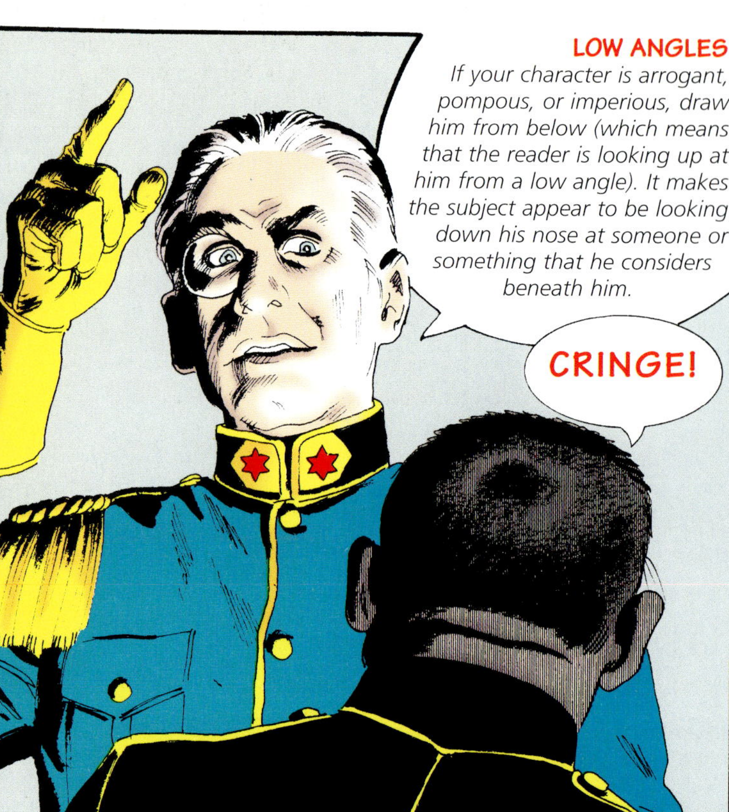

LOW ANGLES *If your character is arrogant, pompous, or imperious, draw him from below (which means that the reader is looking up at him from a low angle). It makes the subject appear to be looking down his nose at someone or something that he considers beneath him.*

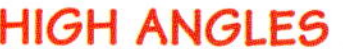

HIGH ANGLES *High angles have the opposite effect, conveying the impression that we are looking down at someone. High angles indicate another character's point of view, also known as a "POV." This picture is drawn from the POV of the guy at the upstairs banister.*

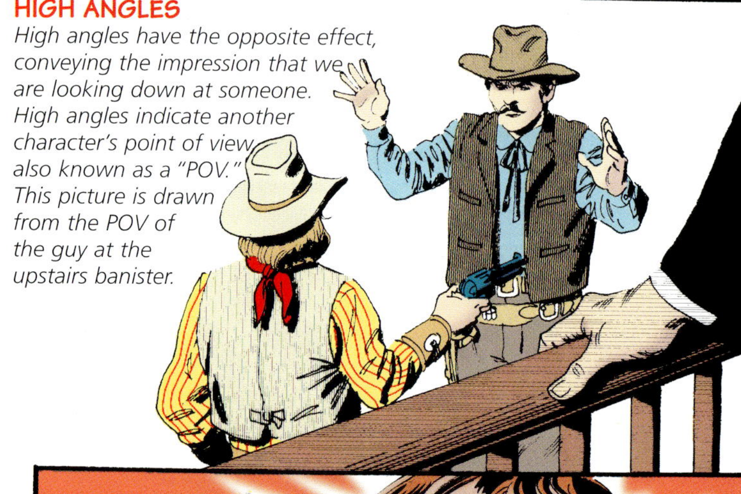

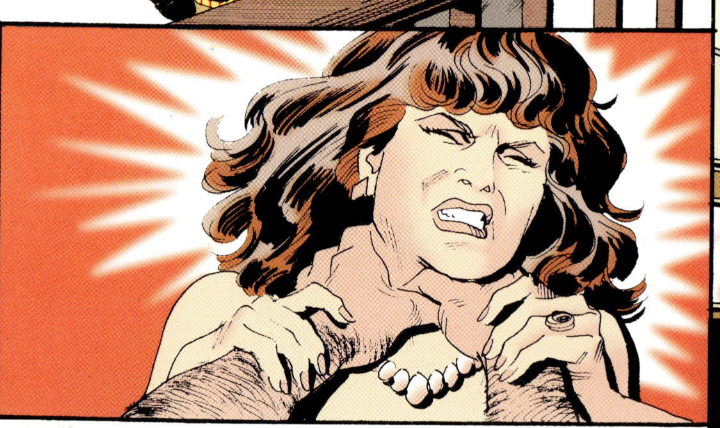

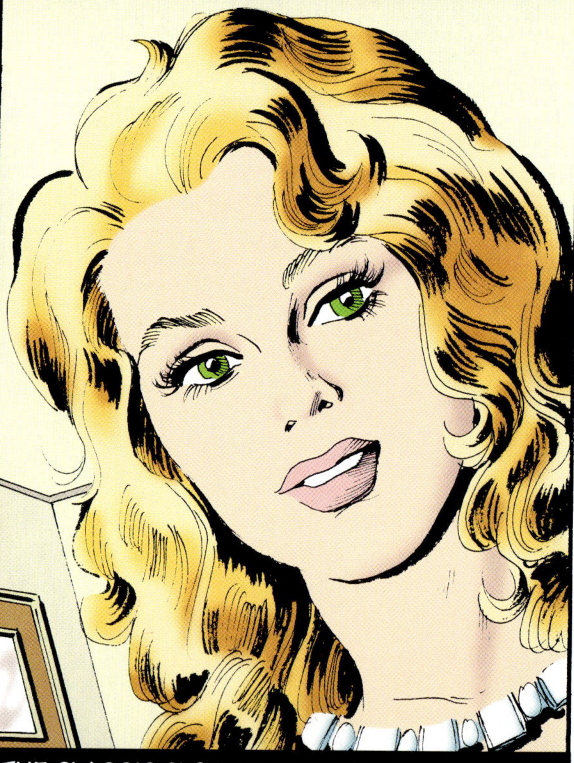

THE CLASSIC CLOSE-UP *is used to focus entirely on your principal without non-essential, distracting extras with exception of a perspective line or two to indicate the background.*

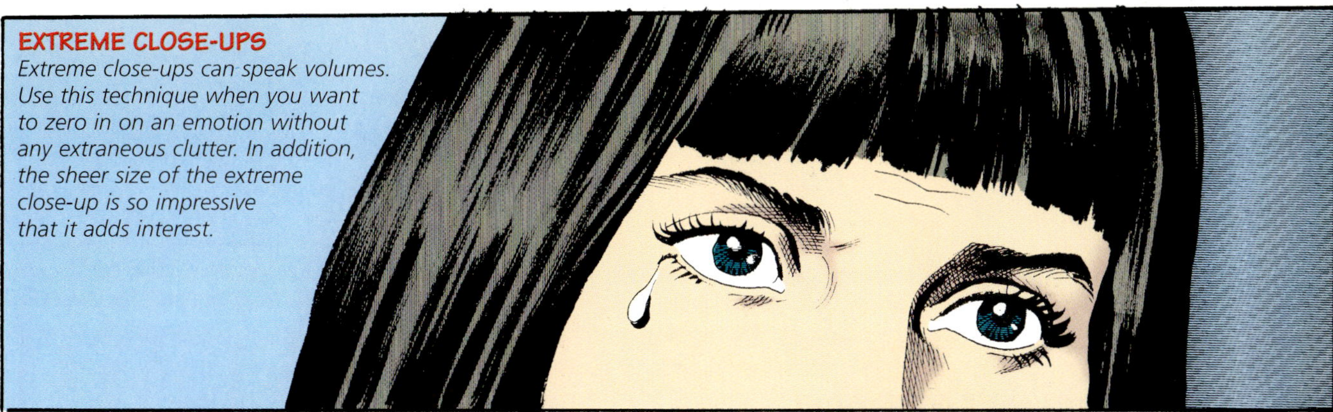

EXTREME CLOSE-UPS

Extreme close-ups can speak volumes. Use this technique when you want to zero in on an emotion without any extraneous clutter. In addition, the sheer size of the extreme close-up is so impressive that it adds interest.

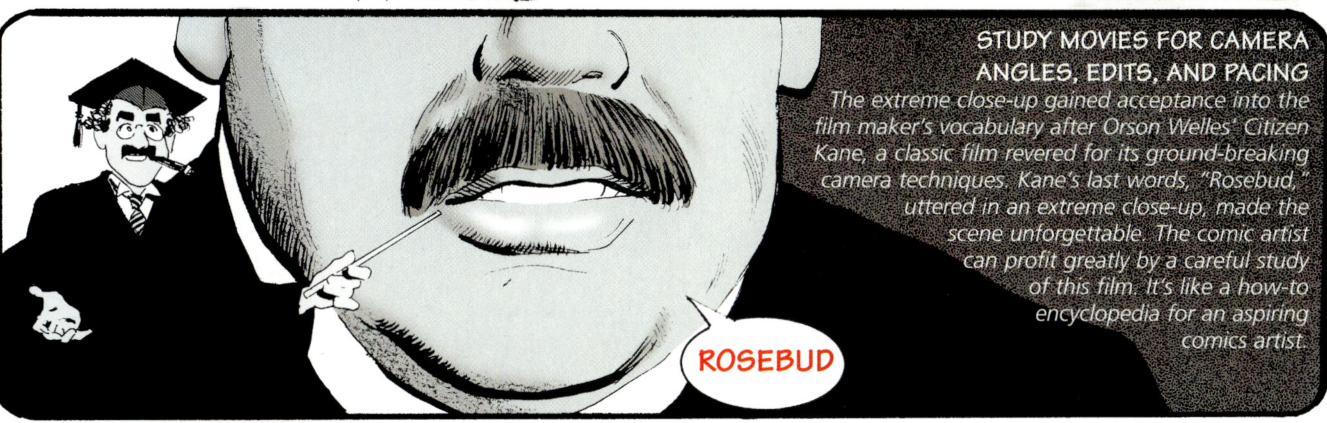

STUDY MOVIES FOR CAMERA ANGLES, EDITS, AND PACING

The extreme close-up gained acceptance into the film maker's vocabulary after Orson Welles' Citizen Kane, a classic film revered for its ground-breaking camera techniques. Kane's last words, "Rosebud," uttered in an extreme close-up, made the scene unforgettable. The comic artist can profit greatly by a careful study of this film. It's like a how-to encyclopedia for an aspiring comics artist.

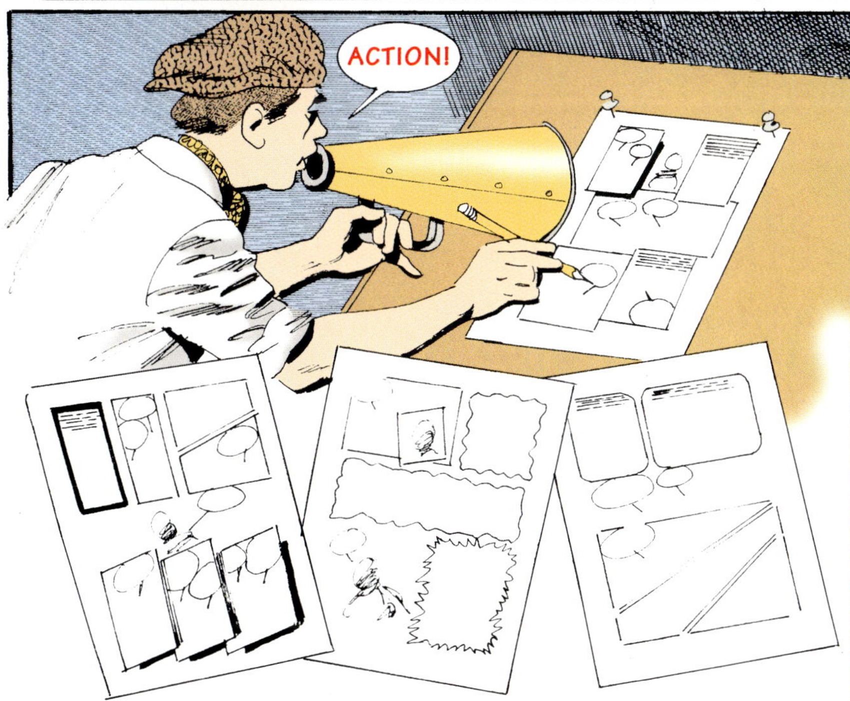

YOU ARE THE DIRECTOR

You may not have a Winnebagoe on the set, or a chair with your name printed on the back of it, but you, too, are a director. You call the angles. You direct the characters. You set the tone.

COMICS INFLUENCE THE MOVIES

Not only have films influenced comics, but comics have had a great impact on films. The "voice-over" shows people speaking while we see the outside of the airplane. This is a technique that comic book artists have been using since before it became a popular film technique. The technique has been expanded to show voice-overs of exterior scenes, beach scenes, and other long shots.

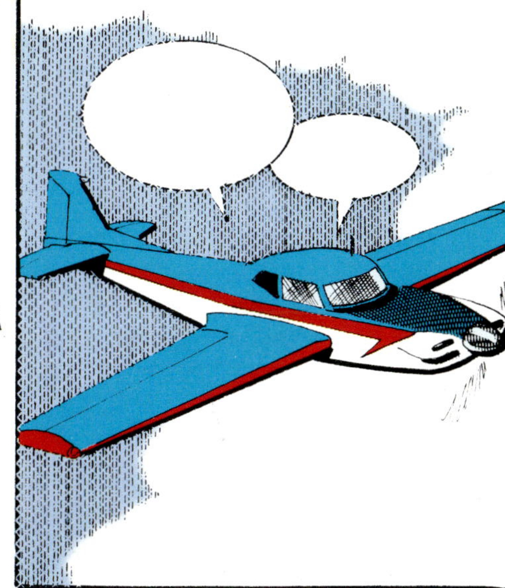

STAGING A SCENE

Talky scenes are worth a panel or two. Comic writers can sometimes overwrite the scenes, making them visually unexciting. One frequent problem for the artist, is what's known in the trade as the "lapel-hanger" page (one of the characters has nothing better to do than hold another character's lapels while delivering his lines). We can use close-ups, long shots, emphasize gestures and expressions, and use lighting and extreme angles to add interest to whatever the script indicates, just as they do in Hollywood.

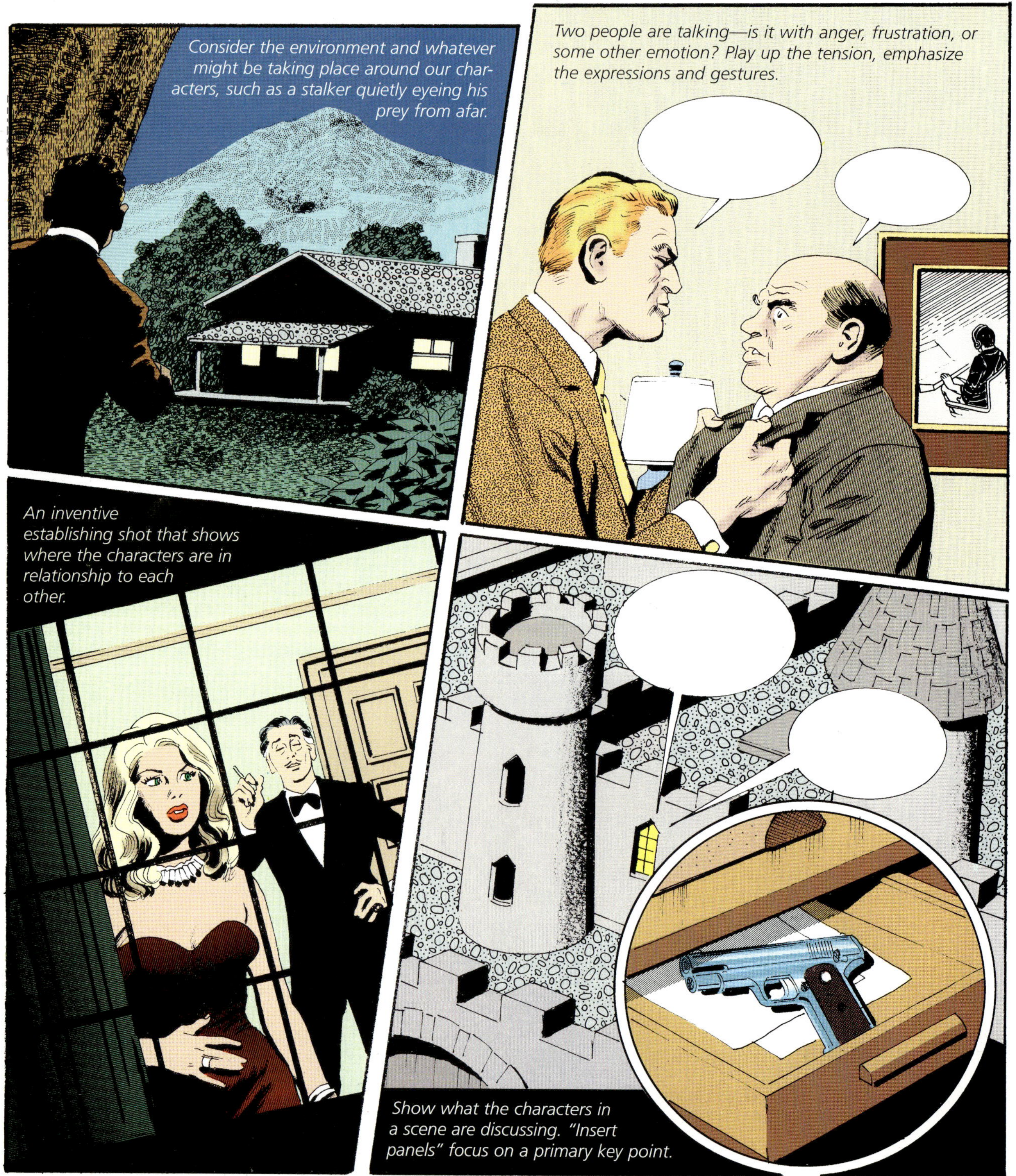

Consider the environment and whatever might be taking place around our characters, such as a stalker quietly eyeing his prey from afar.

Two people are talking—is it with anger, frustration, or some other emotion? Play up the tension, emphasize the expressions and gestures.

An inventive establishing shot that shows where the characters are in relationship to each other.

Show what the characters in a scene are discussing. "Insert panels" focus on a primary key point.

Get the idea? Of course you do. Just do whatever you can to exaggerate and embellish what is basically an ordinary scene with whatever inventiveness and imagination you can inject.

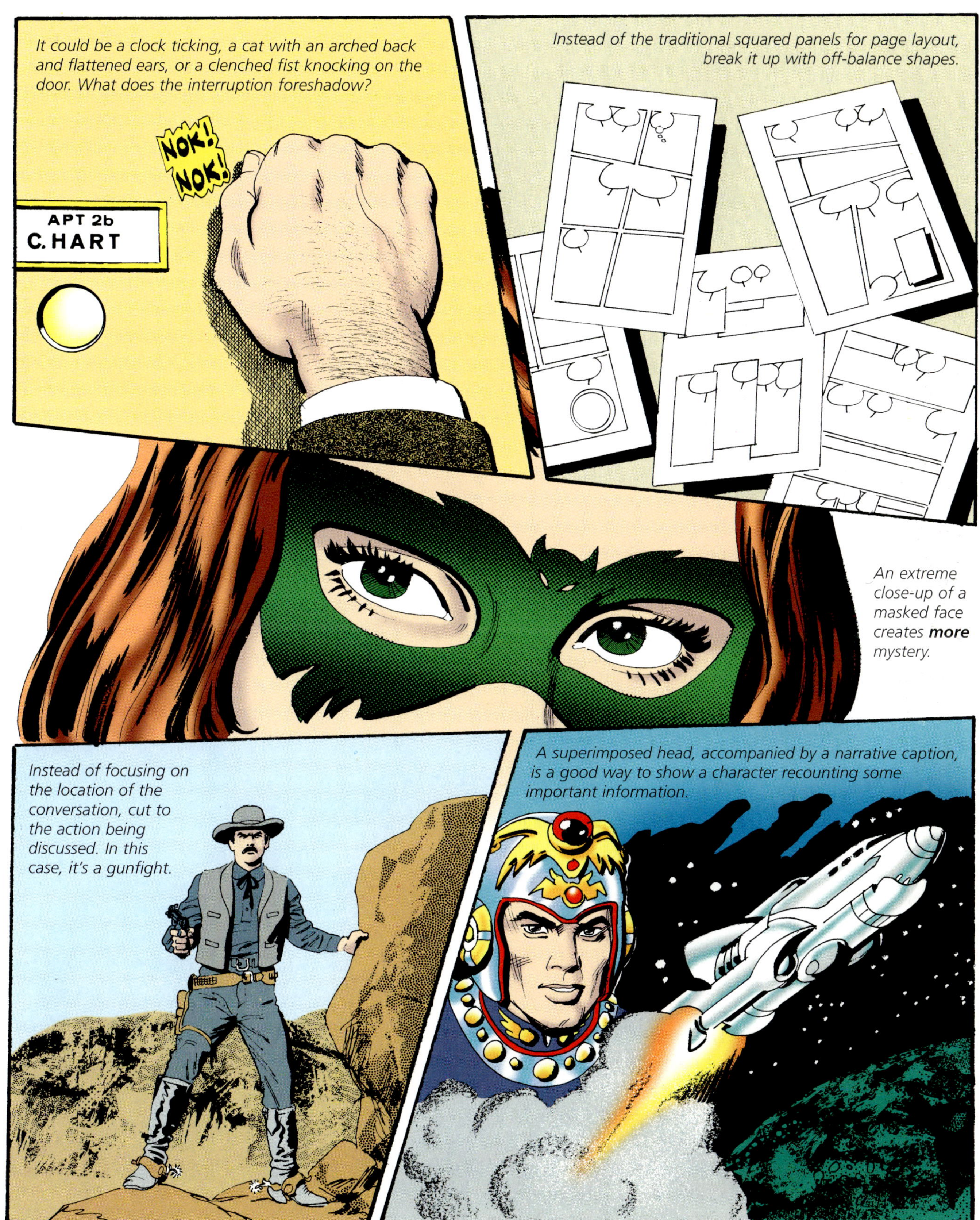

It could be a clock ticking, a cat with an arched back and flattened ears, or a clenched fist knocking on the door. What does the interruption foreshadow?

Instead of the traditional squared panels for page layout, break it up with off-balance shapes.

*An extreme close-up of a masked face creates **more** mystery.*

Instead of focusing on the location of the conversation, cut to the action being discussed. In this case, it's a gunfight.

A superimposed head, accompanied by a narrative caption, is a good way to show a character recounting some important information.

If the scene involves a flashback, you may want to pump up the narrator's importance. Vignettes can focus on an event.

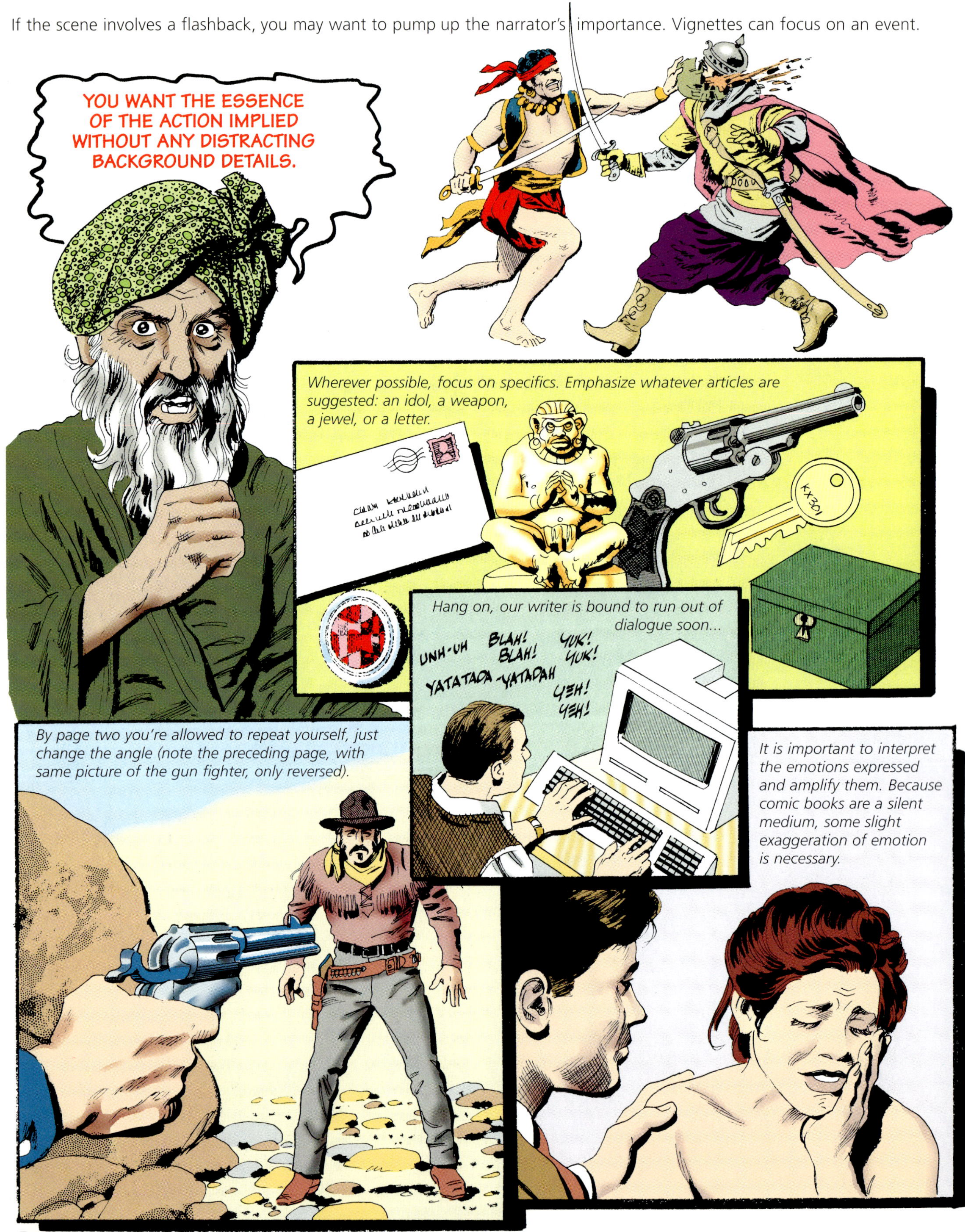

The previous few pages should give you some idea of what to do with a script in which nothing is really happening. Action is the key word. Insert action whenever possible, even if it's only someone pounding a desk or slamming a door. Most people tend to express themselves with their hands. Even the slightest gesture, such as someone stroking his chin, is more interesting than just a talking head!

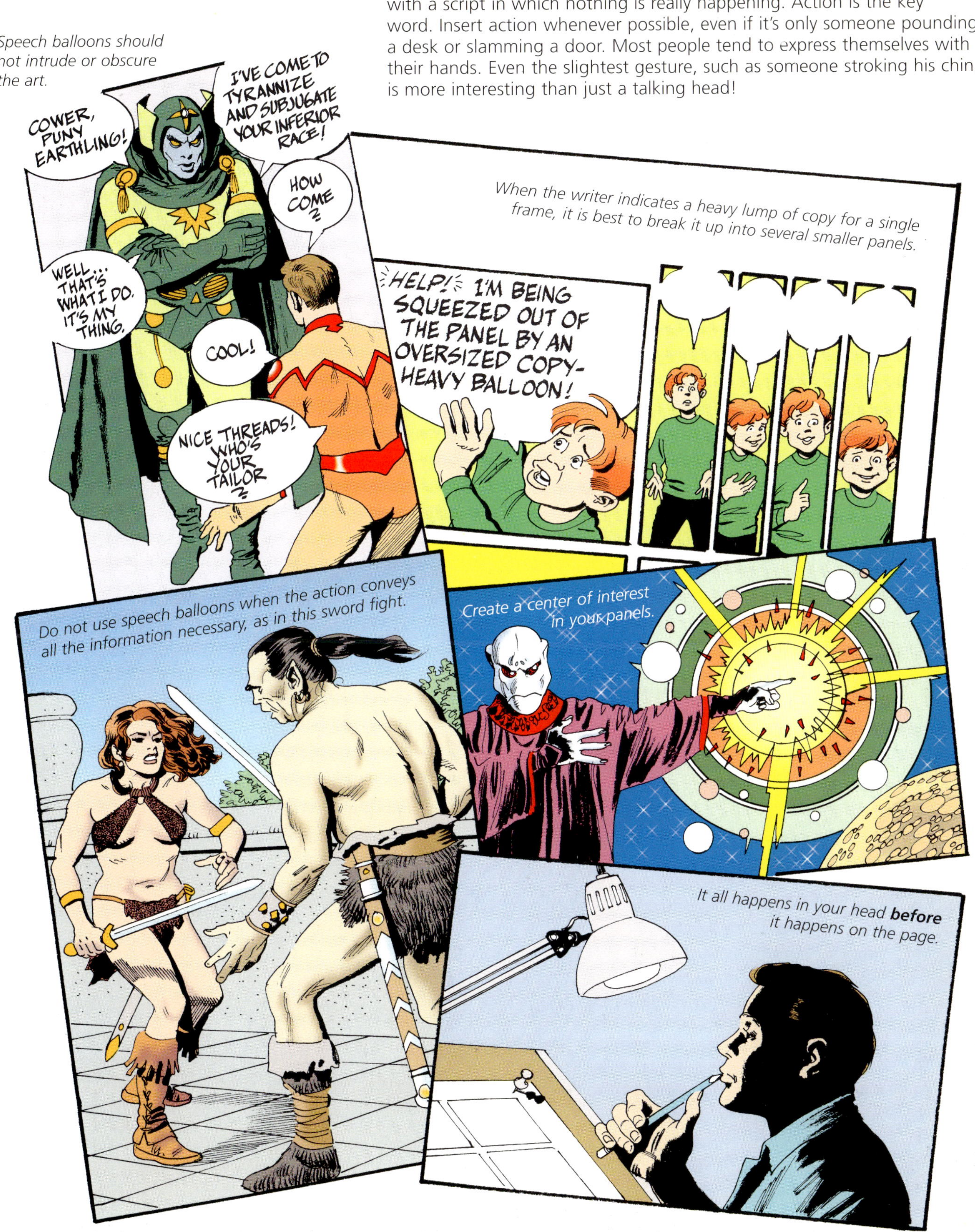

Speech balloons should not intrude or obscure the art.

When the writer indicates a heavy lump of copy for a single frame, it is best to break it up into several smaller panels.

Do not use speech balloons when the action conveys all the information necessary, as in this sword fight.

Create a center of interest in your panels.

*It all happens in your head **before** it happens on the page.*

LET YOUR CHARACTERS SPEAK!

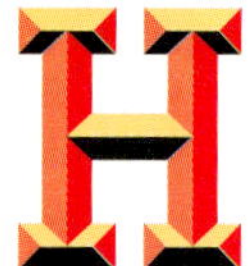

Here are the basic hints that will give you a good foundation in hand-lettering, so that your hard-won efforts to draw aren't undermined by sloppy scrawl in a speech balloon. Much of comic book lettering is done on the computer. Nonetheless, these pointers will help you whether you letter by hand, choose computer fonts, or invent your own typefaces for your comics.

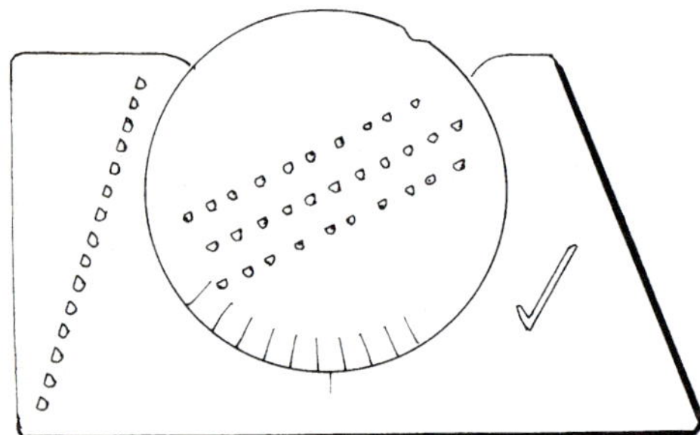

PROFESSIONAL HINT:
The indispensable Ames lettering guide is your main tool. It conveniently gives you the precise parallel lines necessary for your copy.

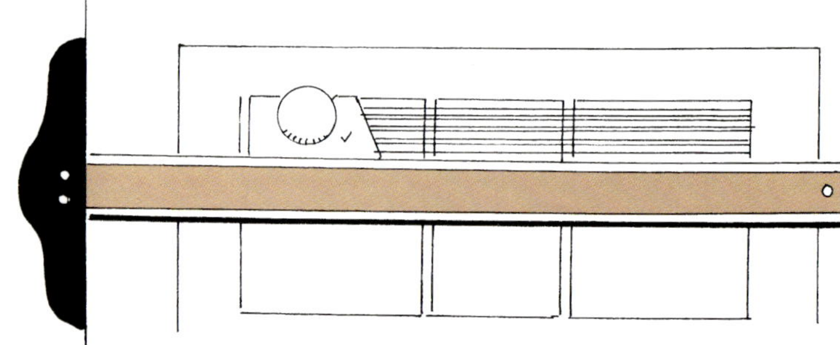

SKETCH GUIDELINES FIRST
Horizontal guidelines are drawn lightly in pencil, then erased after the letters are inked.

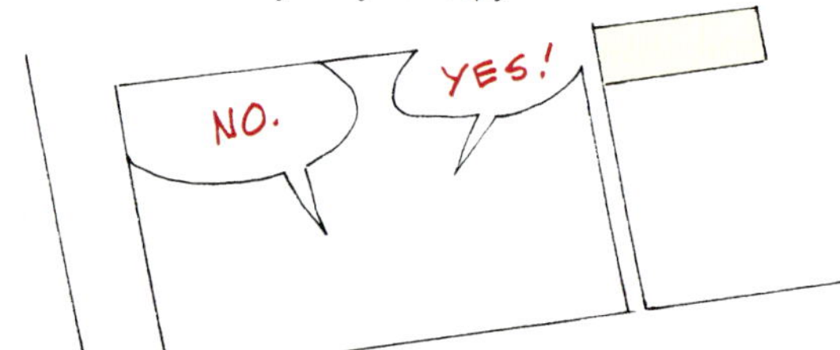

SPEECH BALLOONS AND CAPTIONS
Balloons and captions should occur at the top of the panel and be as unobtrusive as possible. Captions that describe what is occuring in the scene are redundant, and balloons pasted over the art are distracting. Comics are first and foremost a visual medium, and secondarily a literary one. Allow the art room to breath.

THICK & THIN
PEN NIBS
SLANT SLANT
BOLD **BOLDER**
A REVERSE SLANT SOMETIMES INDICATES A FOREIGN TONGUE

PEN TYPES
There are a wide variety of pen nibs available. By experimenting you will find the ones that suit your needs. Some are uniform in strength of line, some offering a thick/thin line due to its spade-like point. Any and all can be found at your local art supply store.

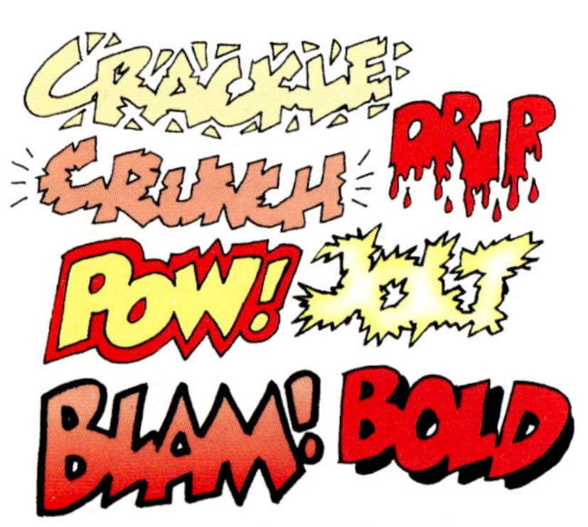

SOUND EFFECTS LETTERING
Sound effects are created by using informal block letters. Block letters can become even more expressive by giving them the visual essence of what they impart, such as cracking, crushing, or booming. Shadows can increase their impact

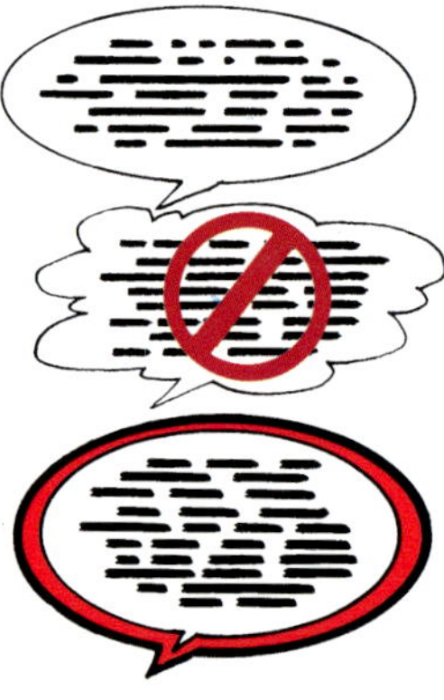

SPEECH BALLOONS
Balloon shapes most pleasing to the eye are rounded or elliptical rather than scalloped. Heavily outlined balloons are an excellent attention grabber.

lower case is sometimes used in narrative captions

YOU'RE NOT RESTRICTED AS TO STYLE AS LONG AS IT'S LEGIBLE AND STILL EASY TO READ IN REDUCTION

style STYLE STYLE
STYLE **STYLE**
STYLE STYLE
STYLE, ETC., ETC....

STYLE
Lettering style is a matter of individual taste. But be sure to keep it consistent, don't change the style halfway through the book.

DYNAMIC PERSPECTIVE

Perspective. Ah yes, the dreaded "P" word. You could try memorizing a long list of rules about perspective, but you'd only end up hating your life. It's far more important that you get a "gut sense" of the three types of perspective used in comic books. Try to identify the types of perspective, as well as the locations of vanishing lines whenever you look at an illustrated scene or even in the real world. Make it a game. You'll start noticing the perspective in everything, not as an academic exercise, but as the integral element of the design that it is. Eventually, it will become instinctive.

ONE-POINT PERSPECTIVE

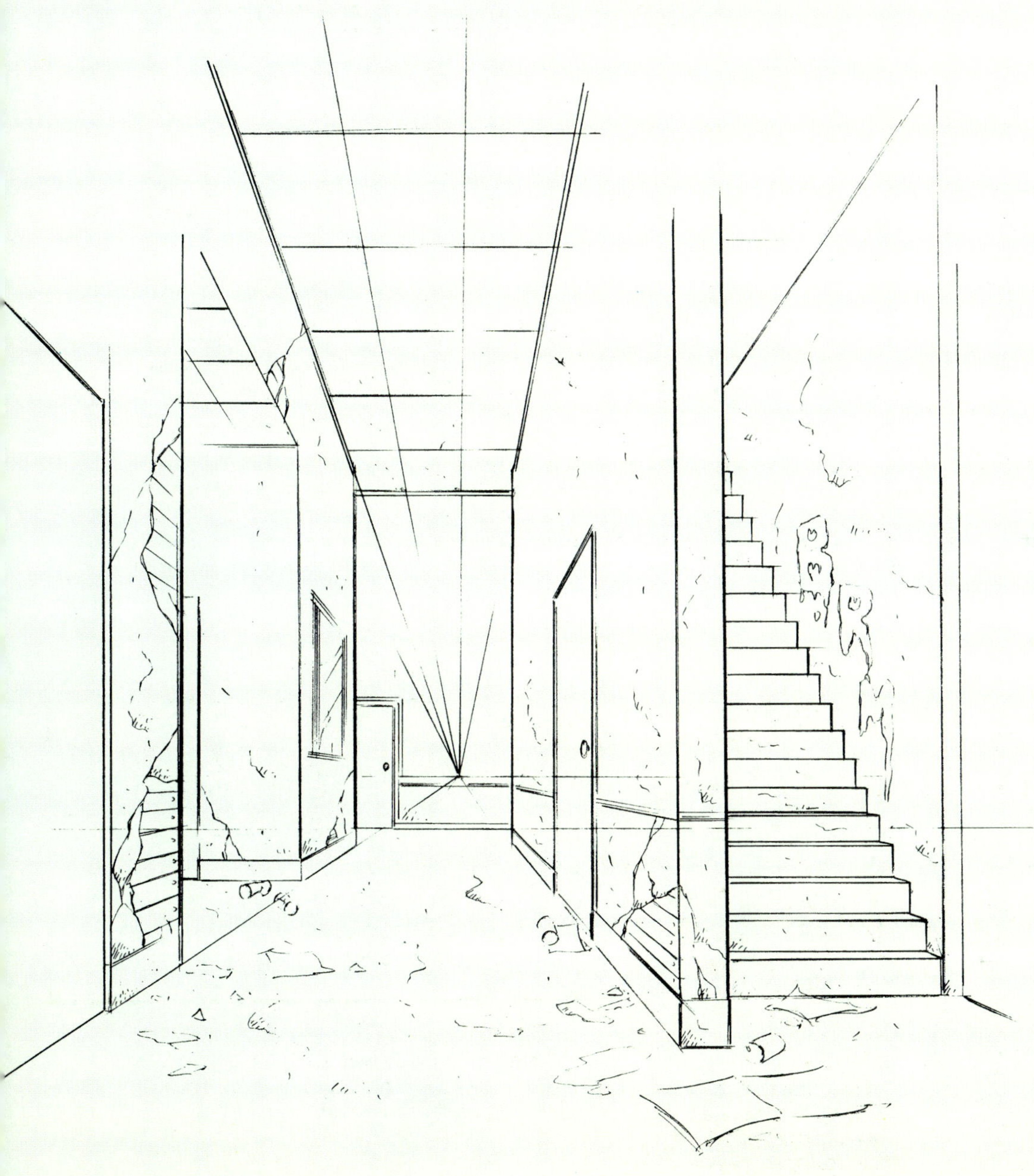

Here's a trick question: How many vanishing points does one-point perspective have? Time's up. The answer is one. Your next question is probably going to be, "What's a vanishing point?" A vanishing point is a single spot where the lines converge. In one-point perspective, the vanishing point is almost always in the middle of the picture.

The lines that appear to be traveling *away* from you *must converge*, because as they get further away, they get closer together until they eventually meet at a single point, much like a railroad tracks appear to do. And that point is called the *vanishing point*.

There are some lines in the picture that are not traveling away from you. They simply drift across the page horizontally, like the treads in the staircase and the vertical lines that go up to the ceiling.

The vanishing lines are merely guidelines that the artist follows, to help him or her to decrease the size of objects as they recede into the background. Look at the drawing for the vanishing point. See the vanishing lines, notice how everything diminishes along them.

TWO-POINT PERSPECTIVE

Two-point perspective occurs when the vanishing point is not in the middle of the picture. Two-point perspective has two vanishing points, one on the left and one on the right. Everything is always converging to either one of these two points. And note that the vanishing point doesn't have to appear inside the picture. These particular points converge somewhere off the picture. You'll develop a good sense of perspective as you begin to understand the principles of vanishing points.

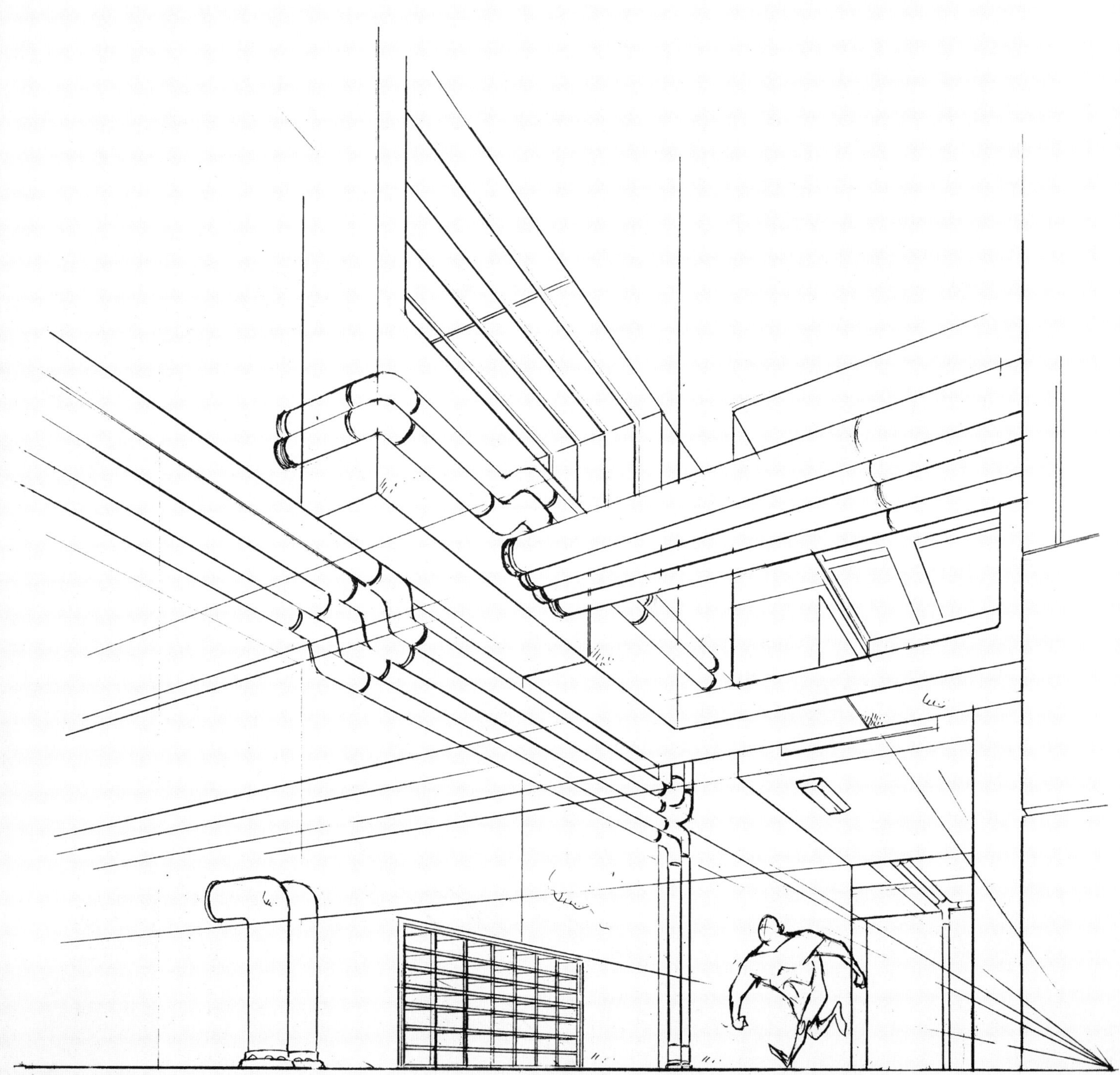

THREE-POINT PERSPECTIVE

Three-point perspective is often used in comics to create dynamic scenes. It's basically two-point perspective with the addition of extreme or exaggerated height, where the reader is either looking up or down at the objects. It can be an exterior scene, as in this example; or an interior setting, as in an atrium, an abandoned warehouse, a huge underground missile silo, or a computer science lab. The possibilities are limitless.

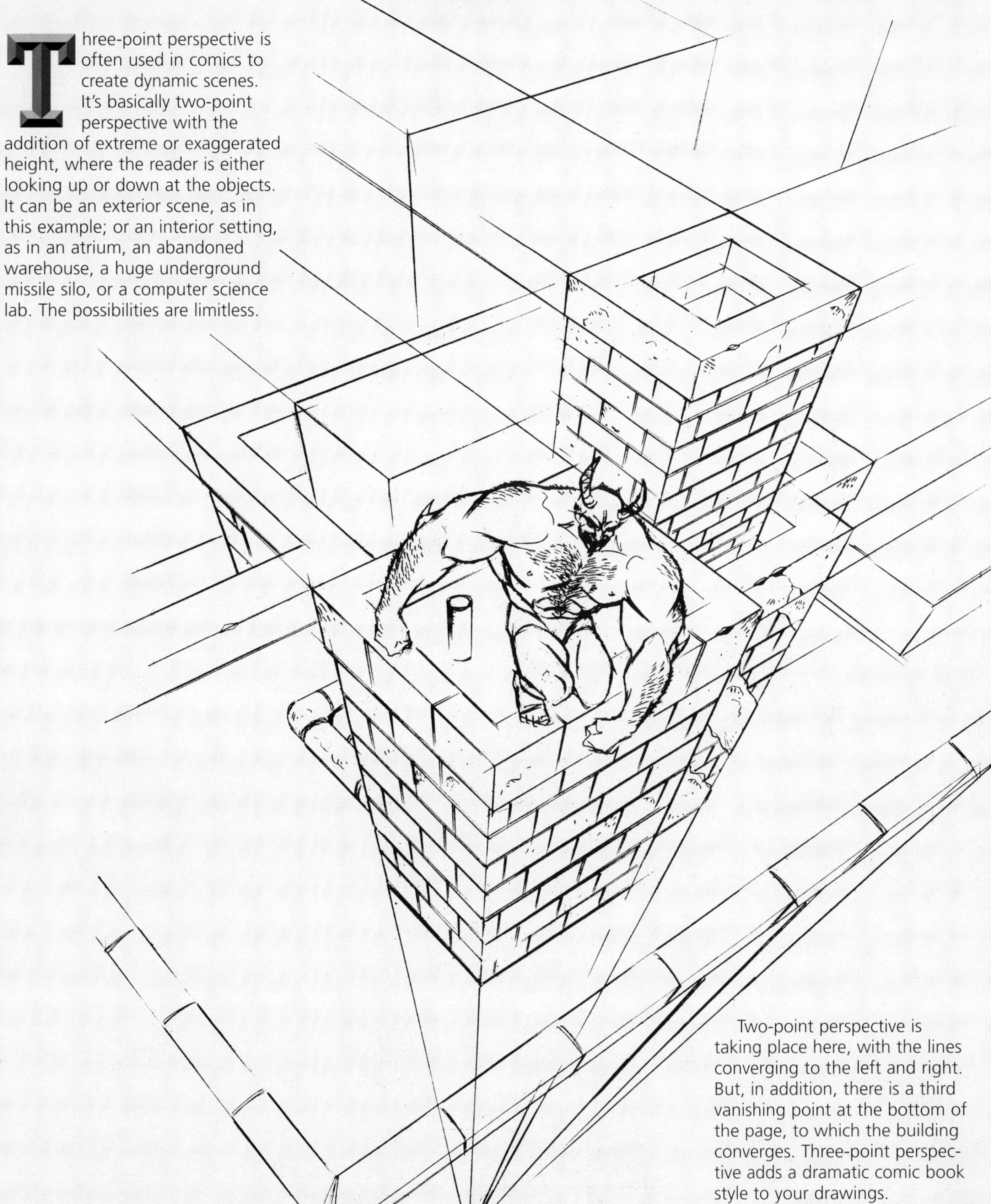

Two-point perspective is taking place here, with the lines converging to the left and right. But, in addition, there is a third vanishing point at the bottom of the page, to which the building converges. Three-point perspective adds a dramatic comic book style to your drawings.

MOODY SETTINGS

Okay, so you're getting the knack of drawing comic book figures. But now that you can draw them, what are you going to do with them? You can draw them flying around in space, blasting each other with alpha rays and the like, but sooner or later you're going to have to put them in a scene on the ground, with a background, in a setting. That's what this section is all about.

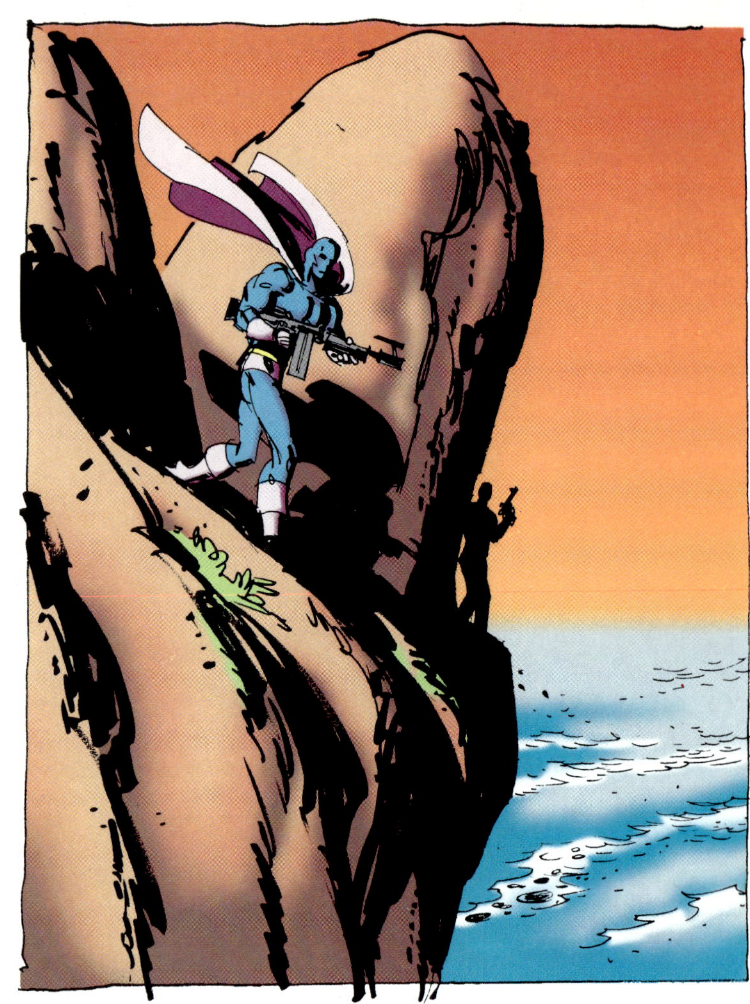

HOW TO EFFECTIVELY SHOW DISTANCE BETWEEN CHARACTERS

Show distance by contrasting the sizes of the figures. The foreground figure is significantly larger than the figure standing in the background. You cannot judge the size of a rock until you put a human figure—or something of known size—next to it. Note the use of light for dramatic effect. The large rock blocks the light source, coming from the left, casting a nice shadow and causing the smaller figure to appear in silhouette. This serves to add contrast between the two figures.

CITYSCAPES AND SILHOUETTES

Cities are a popular backdrop for comic book stories. When you think of cities, don't just think of skyscrapers, but of downtown tenement buildings as well. The overhead train tracks add a bleak, moody feel to the scene. The city is filled with old discarded projects, garbage dumps, alley-ways, broken fire hydrants, and the like. Next time you're in a major city, bring a sketch-pad and make some quick sketches. Create a file of these drawings and you'll never run out of interesting material for backgrounds.

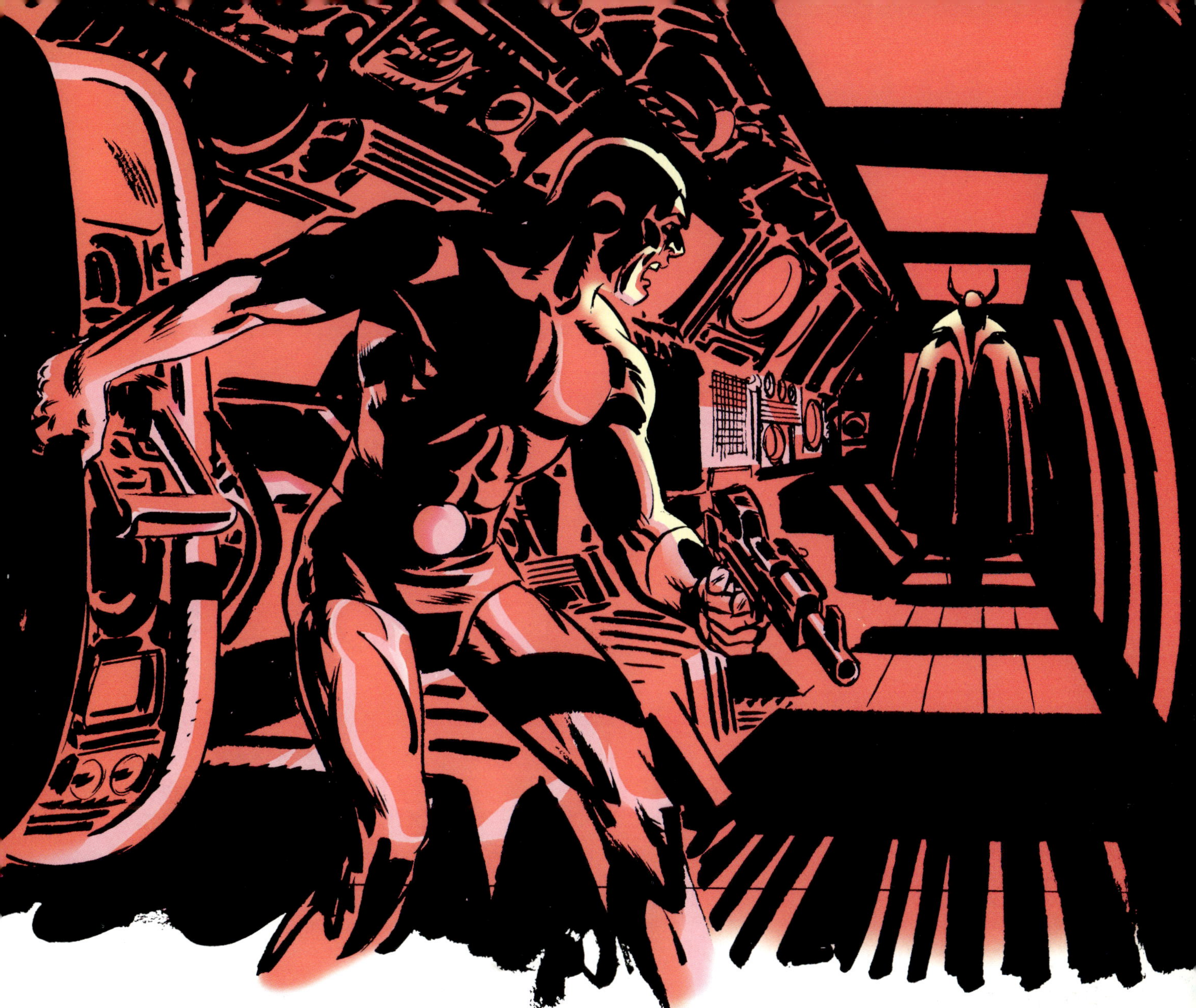

JUXTAPOSING LIGHT AND DARK

With a starship interior, a submarine, or even a science lab, you get a chance to invent your own unique machinery. If it looks like it serves a function, then it works. This illustration is a wonderful example of pools of black positioned inside pools of white; and pools of white inside pools of black. It has a heavily dramatic effect, to be used at the crescendo of a scene. This scene is alive with tension. You can practically hear the bad guy's quiet footsteps getting closer. That weapon the good guy is holding won't be enough.

Look what has been done in this drawing. By the heightened use of black and white, the scene has become so ominous (especially the bad guy), and the situation so dangerous, that we, as readers, don't even believe that the guy holding the gun has the advantage. Now that's prime storytelling!

HOW TO CREATE A FANTASTIC COVER

Here's a professional secret you can use to create dynamic covers. But first lets think about what makes a great cover. Sure, you'll want to see your favorite character featured, but what else? A snappy title. Okay. But what makes it eye-catching? The way the cover elements interact is what makes something catch your eye. Remember, you are competing with fifty other comic books on the wall. You want *yours* to be the one that gets noticed. We want to grab the readers attention and pull him/her in. The cover has to be clear, visually concise, powerful, dramatic, intriguing, and energetic.

To create a visually concise image, a good beginning can be made by using the Letter Design Method. Pick a letter from the alphabet, and create an overall design that mimics shape of the letter.

Once you get more experienced, you can start to create your own designs not based on lettering, but based on an interesting flow of the characters, positioned to bring the eye into the scene.

ROUGH ATTEMPTS

Rough out several attempts before settling on one design and finishing it. Always, *always* do this.

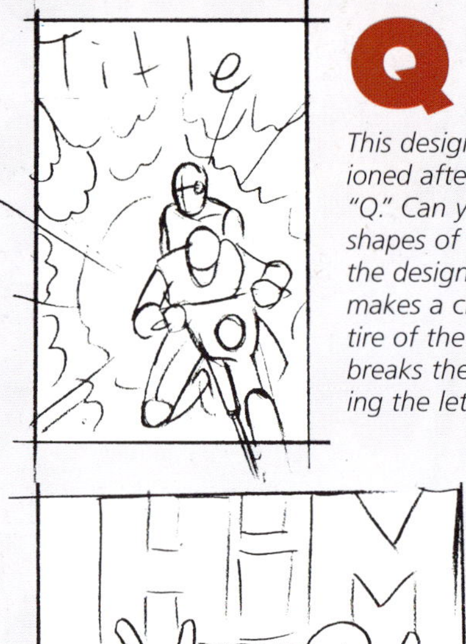

Q

This design was fashioned after the letter "Q." Can you see the shapes of the letter in the design? The blast makes a circle, and the tire of the motorcycle breaks the circle, creating the letter "Q."

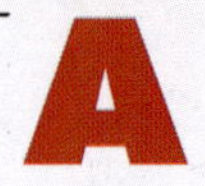

This design resembles the letter "A."

O *This design is loosely based on a circle, formed by the arms and legs of the characters. But it doesn't show the hero's face. What if your reader is looking for his favorite character on the cover, and you don't show his face? You lose the sale. Close, but try again.*

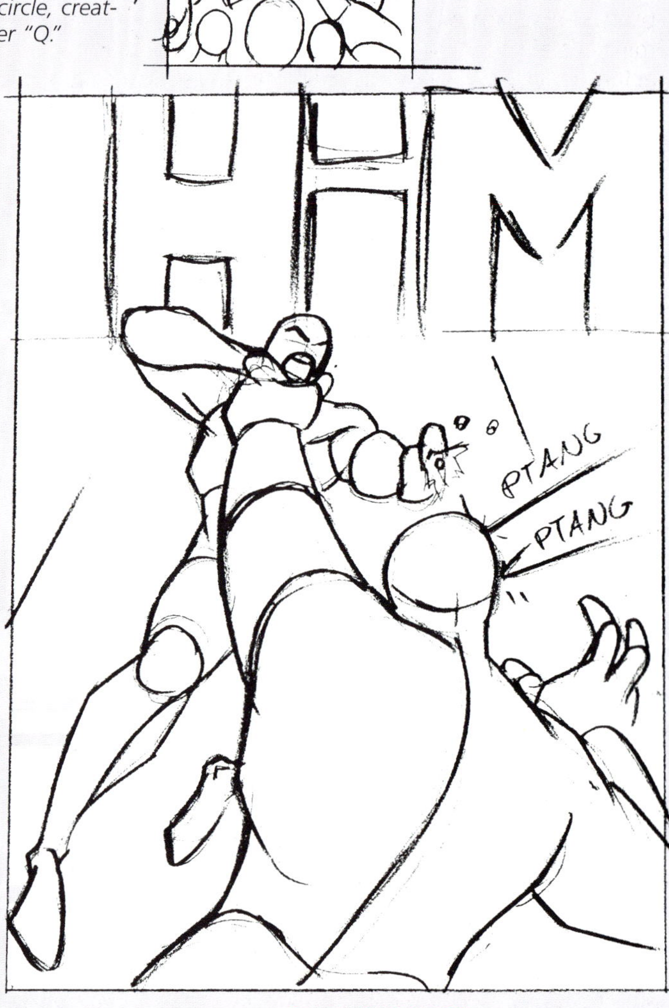

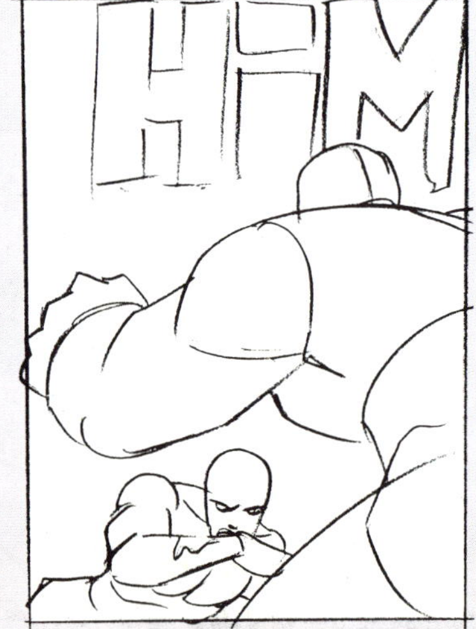

This angle, from behind the bad guy, shows the hero's face. It's interesting, but what happened to the energy? The hero is down in the fight. Sometimes a quiet cover can be good. But in a fight scene, the action should be shown. Hopefully, three's a charm. Next...

THE WINNER!

This is a great cover sketch if I've ever seen one. It's got it all. The hero is in danger, with his face in view, and there's solid composition and action. The arm is leading your eye from the bad guy to the good guy.

Never settle on the first thing that pops into your head. Sometimes you can combine elements from different sketches.